I0817339

PAPER

Techniques & Projects to Sculpt

FLOWER

Your Own Garden of Realistic Blooms

MAGIC

SOFIA VUSIR JANSSON

Photography by Linda Lomelino

Other Schiffer Craft Books on Related Subjects:

Blooming Paper: How to Handcraft Paper Flowers and Botanicals, Laura Reed, ISBN 978-0-7643-6208-8

Flower Delights: 40 Enjoyable Things to Do with Flowers, Sara Princé & Sandrine Tournigand, ISBN 978-0-7643-6310-8

Endless Florescence: Transformative Contemporary Dried Floral Design, Jenny Thomasson, ISBN 978-0-7643-6430-3

Originally published as *Pappersblommor* by Natur & Kultur, Stockholm © 2024 Sofia Vusir Jansson
Translated from the Swedish by Carol Rhoades

Library of Congress Control Number: 2025939866

Cover design by Lindsay Hess
Interior design by Stefan Fält
Back cover design and interior layout by Lori Malkin Ehrlich
Type set in Mercury Text Display, Mercury Text G2, and Scandia Bold
Photography by Linda Lomelino

ISBN: 978-0-7643-7133-2
ePub: 978-1-5073-0640-6
Printed in China

10 9 8 7 6 5 4 3 2 1

Published by Schiffer Craft
An imprint of Schiffer Publishing, Ltd.
4880 Lower Valley Road
Atglen, PA 19310
Phone: (610) 593-1777; Fax: (610) 593-2002
Email: Info@schifferbooks.com
Web: www.schifferbooks.com

Preface

I look around the studio at the flowers surrounding me. It is still remarkable, I think, that I am so connected to flowers. I've always liked flowers—but have never had a green thumb. I remember when my grandmother, long after I became an adult and she was over ninety years old, surprisingly commented that we had geraniums in our window. So it may be logical that my book deals with paper flowers rather than real ones. It is still surprising how life can take unexpected turns.

It has been ten years since I created my first paper flower. The reason was simple: I needed a large-scale flower to photograph. I remember that I chose a large branch for a stem, created the pistil out of a bundle of dried straw, and formed the petals with silk paper.

I found the instructions for constructing a rose with silk paper in a 1915 edition of *Allers Familj-Journal* (Aller's Family Journal). The chapter began with a text explaining that, even if nature can never be measured with a person's hand, a dexterous person can create an art product that almost seems "living." I envision paper flowers the same way. For me, it is obvious that the flower is not real, perhaps because of the dimensions or the artistic freedom in creation. For me, it is a unique art form, handwork that captures the *feeling* of the living and organic in the natural kingdom that sometimes actually surpasses reality.

For me, feeling is the most important in the art of paper flowers. The unique and personal expression is what I most strive for. As for the work itself, I'm not at all interested in depicting reality. In my thinking, it's about the same as not being able to perceive whether an artwork is a photograph or a painting. A work photographed as reality is impressive, but, for me, that is not inspiring.

Therefore, it can feel contradictory if the flowers I have created for this book are simply true to life in form, size, and dimensions. They are my interpretations of flowers you can find in gardens, in nature, and on your windowsill. I want to emphasize that although the flowers are almost realistic, they are my personal interpretations of various species. I am not an expert in botany. For each flower I have created, I did close-up study. I want to understand the flower's shape, construction, and structure, and to find the key to why the flower looks the way it does. I consider the latter as subjective and personal. We all take in different details and meanings as most primary, and we all see reality in different ways.

I often say, "What is perfect is not always the prettiest or most correct." I believe that many times, we are so attached to a type of habitual sight that we do not see things as they really are. Digital tools and industrialization have determined that the perfect and "error-free" are what is pretty, instead of letting us see handcraft and the hand. With interpretation, one can go from the "inner template," which was probably not grounded just in your own thinking but also in something you had been told.

But I still want, despite realism, for us to get the feeling that what we are working with are paper flowers. Feel free—it's what I do.

Introduction

Paper flowers are neither new nor modern. Nor are they specifically Swedish (my home country) or bound to any one country. Right now, and as far back as the nineteenth century, you'll find paper flowers in cultures all over the world, both in folk traditions and in art.

Earlier, paper flowers were used the same way as we use fresh flowers today: as decoration for festivities, parties, weddings, baptisms, and funerals. These flowers were not only a durable alternative to fresh but often the only option for flower decorating. They were most obvious during the times of the year when fresh flowers were expensive or difficult to obtain.

We know that in earlier times, both festive and sorrowful occasions could stretch over several days and that people did not have the flower beds and nurseries that we have today. Flower shops here in Sweden first appeared at the beginning of the twentieth century. Earlier, only those well off enough to have their own gardeners and gardens could afford to decorate their homes with cut flowers.

Handcrafters specializing in the art of paper flowers worked in studios in the larger cities. They made flowers with both fabric and paper, but paper flowers were considered the most exclusive. Perhaps it was their beauty and their impermanence that made them so particularly treasured. People even handed in their flowers for periodic maintenance and repair, an act that feels very distant in today's consumer society. Today, it seems as if a large part of the population prefers cheap decorations that won't make a dent in their wallet, something to throw away after a season, and then it's off to buy something new for the next season.

At the same time as there were studios in the cities for making the more exclusive flowers, a strong tradition flourished in the countryside where people made paper flowers with recycled materials they had on hand. This handcraft was part of festive and special times before each of the year's celebrations, when people gathered to prepare decorations. I have often thought that this was the actual meaning for decorations, not just their aesthetic appeal—that the time before the event, with companionship and a feeling of contributing to something, was at least as valuable as what we would later rest our eyes on for a short time. The techniques spread from generation to generation and developed over time. The flowers were simple in form and look, which meant that all ages could contribute and that people could produce a large amount in a short time. Maybe the more monotonous aspects of the craft even provided peace of mind and quiet, just as crafting can be an escape from today's stress.

At the end of the nineteenth century, patterns for flowers became common. Not least, paper flowers were used on the Christmas tree and are actually one of our oldest Christmas decorations. At that time, weekly journals were filled with descriptions of botanic decorations both imaginative and realistic. Legend says that winter flowers bloomed on Christmas night, and the tree was filled with a colorful mix of all kinds, like a wintertime flower meadow.

Finding articles that confirm what I have heard is like putting a puzzle together. On the back of a book published in 1858, which I found at a second-hand bookstore, it says: "The lovely art of making paper and fabric flowers has already become a favorite hobby for our young women and it deserves to become more generally known, now when both crochet and netting have gone out of style." The 1858 book featured pictures of tools and templates for common flowers such as buttercups and poppies but also mentioned flower names that are no longer familiar today. The templates themselves are not particularly interesting to me, but the text is wonderful and entertaining. Measurements were not given, but, instead, recommendations such as the "width of a straw." The author pointed out that one works primarily with the right hand; the left hand was considered a complicated alternative for anyone trying. There were recipes for floral glue and warnings that aqua regia is corrosive. One could buy bottles of ready-made sky blue, a color excellent for flowers that could decorate a ball dress. There was also a description for a rose that could be made in a minute, but the description of the process is three pages long. Of course, there is a long list of the meanings of various flowers, because they were the emojis of the period.

Handwork

In the foreword, I mentioned that making flowers that are precise copies of real ones is uninteresting to me. That clearly will be obvious in my paper flowers. Still, the flowers in this book are realistic or similar to actual flowers. How does that correspond?

The reasoning is that the best way to learn and understand the handcraft of making paper flowers "correctly" is to begin with our actual flowers. Let me explain why.

To do well with a handcraft requires respect for and understanding of the knowledge and skills connected to it. It means understanding the qualities as well as the limitations and potentials of the materials. But it also requires the ability to see the whole picture, so you can exercise your sense of aesthetics and form. I want to be clear that this does not mean setting the bar too high. Nor does it mean lovely or ugly, right or wrong. When I teach classes, everyone is welcome, even beginners. Understanding a handcraft is a lifelong journey of learning and researching. Every mistake and step forward contribute to development. No matter whether you are a beginner or are experienced, it is most important to really like what you are doing and to be curious. Allow yourself to be creative.

Having respect for handcraft means to dare to trust your own hands and brain, and to use tips and tricks to strengthen your self-confidence as well as to awaken and maintain the desire to continue. In the end, your personal creations will grow and develop.

With the doing itself comes the wordless knowledge—the physical experience when you can feel the materials with your hands, look at what is before you, and listen to how certain movements sound and how the tools have their own melody, depending on how and where you use them. In the making, you will welcome errors and mistakes, which will give you a deeper understanding and open you up to new ideas. I consider this handwork aspect to be crucial for fully mastering your handcraft and for continuing to develop.

My own handwork has developed through the years. I am certified in hairdressing. I have much to be thankful for because this has been very meaningful for my creative development and for my ability to handle tools such as scissors. I worked mostly during the 1990s, when hairdressing was altogether other than natural and dyeing techniques were very advanced. Hair is primarily concerned with innovation and creativity, which taught me a color theory and structure. I was very influenced by Vidal Sassoon and spent a large part of my time in specialized schools grounded in his philosophy. Sassoon's idioms, characterized by geometric shapes, exact lines, and pure precision, are technically exacting. His stylings were built on symmetrical lines, and precise angles with a deep understanding of balance, proportions, structure, and details. Sassoon was strongly influenced by architecture and modern art, which are clearly reflected in his cutting techniques. I believe that it is precisely this deep understanding and respect for handwork that is crucial for self-confidence in handcrafts, no matter whether it is hair or paper flowers.

It is important to understand how your hands function—their shape, movements, and strength are unique to you. This became obvious when I produced thousands of flowers in handwork projects. My hands and the hands of others will not produce the same results even when using the same techniques. During the process of making, when identical products are created, certain techniques will require specific tools to reinforce the steps.

Understanding the value and meaning of handcraft does not just mean copying a pattern or recipe but also really understanding what you are doing. At times I've seen that people think they've reached a goal if they created something exactly as pictured, with, for example, a pattern. But I think that the pattern or "recipe" is there to open up your personal creativity and offer a path so you'll dare to go *further* on the creative journey.

Within the handcraft of making paper flowers, knowledge of how the flower grows and its anatomy is necessary. You need to understand the various parts of the flower, its structure and arrangement, what is specific for each flower and how they are differentiated. The placement of the petals is one of the most important steps for getting flowers that can be recognized as a specific art. The best way to learn this is through creating flowers that are true to life. There is no better area to begin from, to draw both knowledge and inspiration from; the real world of flowers is magic. Sometimes, I'm tempted to say that the complexity of flowers surpasses reality. Just look at the iris and acacia in this book as you learn to create.

The flowers in the book were specifically chosen for their combination of techniques, materials, and construction, as well as interpretations of form and structure to plant a dynamic grounding for learning this handcraft.

I usually divide paper flowers like this:

The "puttered" paper flower: The puttering around is completely free—in this type of flower, you usually don't look at specific techniques, but, instead, you get up close to the material and study it. Once my husband said that to putter is about the same as jamming in music, a creative process completely guided by the imagination.

The simple paper flower: Here you'll use templates and basic techniques but will skip over advanced pistils and details such as sepals and green leaves. It is just sketching the bare contours. This way, you can, relatively quickly, create the feeling of a specific flower and gain an understanding of balance, shape, and construction. This level is an excellent beginning so that next time, you can take another step and add the pistils and other details.

The realistic paper flower: Most of the flowers in this book, with a few exceptions, start at this level. When you follow the instructions, you'll encounter the various parts that are inspired by and interpreted from actual flowers. The dimensions and proportions are suitable for reflecting reality, as is the arrangement of petals, sepals, and leaves. You need to work at this level if you want to learn the basics of handcraft and go on to further develop your paper flower skills.

The detailed paper flower: The next step is to work with coloring, shading, and other details. The book includes a chapter on various coloring techniques and gives tips for the details in certain projects. This is where you'll come closer to your own personal expressions, and so I don't want to steer your choices. For that reason, I put the focus on techniques and the anatomy of flowers, which I consider the basis of handcraft.

The personal expression: Reaching this last step is really the beginning of the journey. It's also the most fantastic part of paper flowers. I often hear that my flowers feel like a heightened version of reality. That's exactly what is so wonderful about paper flowers.

The most important aspect of learning is to learn to feel the materials and how the tools coordinate with them. It is unbelievably time consuming, but it's the most essential process to develop so that you'll be able to take your making forward. Over the years, I've worked with many different materials and with tools that differ, and I'm conscious that this time does not go quickly. But it must be done. Many parts are personal because they rely on everything from the physical to how the brain functions. Also, the large amount of time it takes does not mean that this learning becomes easy or happens automatically. I regard this time as one of the most rewarding parts of creative work, but also as one of the most challenging. To not do anything at all would be the only choice that can hinder me and hinder my development, but, in spite of that fact, I don't want to assert that it is always easy.

I think that understanding the possibilities and limits of the materials is the basis for creative making and is key in how you continue to develop your ideas. I believe in exploring a craft, and that we learn by endless doing and experimenting. When people talk about creativity, many describe it as a flow where solutions fall into place. I feel most creative when things are a little sluggish and contrary, when to solve something I am really forced to go outside my comfort zone. For me, creativity is not knowing where I am going, not having any idea of where I will land. Simply put, it is to completely rely on the process.

How to Use This Book

I recommend that you begin by reading through the chapter on tools and materials (page 18). The best way to learn is by using your hands. If you've never made a paper flower before, I suggest that you begin by trying out several basic techniques. Work without expectations, skipping precise measurements, and, instead, focus on getting comfortable with the materials and tools. Then the next step is to understand the construction of the flower and to choose a simple flower; for example, a sweet pea or a rose. Don't include such advanced parts as the pistil, sepal, or green leaves. The more you learn, the more parts you can gradually add.

Creating paper flowers is exactly like any other type of creating—it can be approached from various levels. You can make very simple versions, like a fun puzzle, and that still counts as a paper flower. On the other hand, you could also make advanced, detailed flowers with intricate coloring, where the creation of a single flower might take several days.

Many people are afraid of making mistakes. I'm precisely the opposite—I love making mistakes. That is exactly what gives the process a forward motion. I am most creative with mistakes. When something goes a little bit wrong is when the solutions come. If I only did what I can already do well, the results would all look the same all the time. That would certainly make me really good at one thing, but it would not make me creative.

It is quite important, though, to understand what is right or wrong. When teaching workshops, I never say that someone's expression or shaping is wrong, even if they have not followed the steps I've been teaching. The only time I step in and make changes is if I see that the end result won't be functional, that the flower will simply fall apart.

Anatomy of a Paper Flower

Understanding the anatomy of a paper flower simplifies the process because then you know how the various parts should be placed.

Pistil: This is always the first part you add to the stem. You should consider it as the center of the flower. It can be visible or hidden, shaped like a ball, a drop, or fringe. The pistil might consist of one or more parts and can be simple or detailed. If you want to speed up the process, the pistil can be simplified without affecting the overall look.

Stamen: This is placed directly adjacent to the pistil. Even if you can buy ready-made stamens, I would never do that. I always make them with paper, by hand.

Petals: The petals are the most visible and what immediately helps you understand what flower it is. They can be made with a variety of paper types and techniques. Focus on the shape, size, and placement, because they are what most often gives the flower its particular look.

Sepal: The sepal sits below the petals, for a fine finish before the flower transitions to the stem. Sepals always hide the attachment at the base, an aspect you need to keep in the back of your mind when assembling the flower.

Stem: The only aspect of my flowers not made of paper is the stem, with its core of steel wire. True, there are ready-made paper-covered steel wires, but it's a good idea to know how to wrap them yourself. You will benefit from that, by learning how to choose the colors for your stem as well as how to join several stems.

Bud: Adding buds gives flowers a dynamic. They can be made easily and are often based on a round or oval shape.

Green leaves: These leaves are placed directly on the stem or on a separate stem that's then attached to the main stem.

Constructing a Flower

Paper flowers are usually constructed from the inside out. The construction of a realistic flower often begins with a stem and a pistil, followed by the petals, the sepal, and, finally, the leaves. The pistils and petals might consist of several layers. To make the work easier, I recommend that you prepare all the parts before you begin assembly. Some color can be applied after the flower has been constructed, but in that case, dry color is used.

The three parts of the pistil are made with recycled paper and shaped like small beads. The paper beads are then covered with crepe paper and glued securely to a short piece of steel wire.

The stamens consist of laminated strips cut into fringe. The tops are given structure with ground semolina.

The stems are wrapped with a paper strip cut against the grain, after the pistil and stamens have been mounted at the top.

Nine petals are cut out and shaped before being glued in two layers around the lower part of the pistil.

The sepal consists of six rounded petals as well as four ovals. The rounded petals form the first layer nearest the stem, while the ovals form the outermost and last layer. Finally, the leaves are attached along the stem.

Tools

0 1 2 3 4 5 6 7 8 9 10 11 12 13 14 15 16 17 18 19
Coccoina
8 SOSTRENE GRENE
7 SOSTRENE GRENE
22 Raphaël

In earlier times, there were specific tools for flower making. I've found pictures of the old tools that were used, and it strikes me how little difference there is between them and the tools used in other handcrafts, at least those tools that are older versus newly manufactured. The tools are the same; they were used, for example, to cut, bend, and shape in various ways.

For the most part, you don't need more than a handful of tools. During my years of creating, I've found that tools sometimes must be discovered, because the shape of our hands influences the end results of the technique. At those times, I went to my husband with a request, and he then developed a tool for a specific technique. That said, when the flower isn't part of a large-quantity production, your own hands and sharp scissors will function excellently.

I am the first to agree that craftwork can give you pain. Suddenly you have gone beyond the limit of what your hands can do. Maybe you get pain in your fingers; I've actually had abrasions from scissors. An arm can go numb or a shoulder aches. So, it's important to take breaks, work in a relaxed mode, and, most of all, understand how you should hold your tools.

Many times, I've just used something near at hand as a tool. Qualities such as shape, surface, and weight influence the materials you work with, and, in fact, most often you don't need anything specially made to take you to the next step. This does mean understanding what you want to do and what you will do it with.

Scissors

Personally, I love cutting. I consider it necessary to learn how to handle scissors. It always helps to have fine motor skills. Research has shown that knowing overall how to use a tool, as an extension of your own arm, is connected with how we learn language and take in knowledge. When you use your hand, the "hand's area" grows in your brain and affects other abilities in the synapses' flow.

I am sometimes questioned about how a child learns to use scissors. There is nothing that is simpler—the child needs a piece of paper and a pair of scissors. Personally, I think that even a young child can learn how to handle a relatively sharp pair of scissors. Blunt, so-called children's, scissors can sometimes make cutting more difficult. Let the child cut freely without a template, folds, or lines. It scares me that learning how to handle tools and working with the hands has been deprioritized. There are many advantages to being able to handle a tool, even as simple as scissors, as a skill useful for the rest of one's life.

As long as paper has been around, people have cut it for aesthetic purposes. It could be a silhouette cutout, a way to tell a story, or a letter. In most cases, the art of paper cutting involves folding the paper and then cutting. Even if someone is a skillful paper cutter, one cannot be totally sure about the end results. The allure is always the surprise at the result, no matter whether it's for a paper flower, a snowflake, or a silhouette depiction.

Sharp, good-quality scissors should never be underestimated. When it comes to paper flowers, a good cutting technique is the basis for a good flower, no matter how difficult your piece is. Dull scissors that don't fit well in your hand will make your handwork difficult and will try your patience. Scissors that will work best for your hand are a personal choice. I recommend three different sizes for your scissors. The tip should be pointed on all of them, and it's a big advantage if you can sharpen your scissors. You need scissors with larger blades to cut large surfaces and to be able to make longer cuts in one snip. That makes for cleaner edges and a more effective way of working. In addition, you'll need a pair of scissors with short blades and very pointed tips for fine details. Medium-sized scissors are also useful. A benchmark for blade sizes is 5¼, 6¾, and 8¼ in. (13, 17, and 21 cm).

There are many brands of scissors on the market, but I recommend those made by Fiskars, particularly those in their Renew series. They're manufactured with 80% recycled materials and 13% new materials and are 100% recyclable. The handles are ergonomic and will fit many hands. They are also easy to sharpen and cost-efficient.

I would also like to remind you about left-handed scissors. My daughter is left-handed but has always cut with scissors for right-handed people. Sometimes in workshops, I teach participants who can cut only with scissors made for the left-handed. Once, I noticed that a participant had trouble keeping up with the course. Her cutting was slow and complicated. I carefully asked if she was left-handed because she had so much trouble with the scissors. She said she'd always had that problem—and she was forty-two years old. When I gave her a pair of left-handed scissors, it was like turning a switch on: She could cut wonderfully.

Dowels

Metal and wood dowels of various dimensions are useful for many things. They are the tools, after scissors, that I use most often. They're perfect for shaping, bending, separating, and applying glue. If you are going to try using a dowel, I recommend one with a dimension of approximately ⅝ in. (1.5 cm).

Ball stylus

This ball-shaped tool contributes to an even cupping without using your fingers. By twisting the tool centered on the cupping and supported by your palm, you can make an even bowl shape.

Ruler

A ruler for measuring is a necessary tool. You can also use a ruler to fold against for sharp, straight lines.

Pliers

You'll need ones with nippers to cut the wire, along with bending it.

Tweezers

Tweezers can function like an extra hand when you need to move small details.

Clamps

Clamps are used like an extra hand for holding shapes together and gluing on leaves. You also need a clamp for leaf techniques.

Spatula

You can control the spread of glue by using a spatula. Most of all, though, it's useful when you are applying larger amounts of glue and for flat bonding.

Materials and Techniques

Crepe Paper

For this book, I exclusively used crepe paper. It's a fun and easy paper to use for flower making. Having it in your hands is a little like rolling a stress ball. It is very malleable and thus very satisfying. It's an extremely durable paper that you can shape repeatedly, making new forms. Several of my flowers have been rented out for various events over the years, and even though they might be damaged between events, I can easily repair them so they look brand new.

What differentiates various types of crepe paper is not only the weight but the elasticity. Once you work with paper, you'll eventually decide on your own favorites. I can recommend different types of paper, but you should feel free to use what you prefer. I exclusively use paper from Werola in Germany and Cartotecnica Rossi in Italy. Both operate with conservation in mind for paper production and dyeing, and they offer transparency concerning their manufacturing processes. This book's projects focus on the Italian paper. The color codes given in the respective flower instructions refer to this paper, with one exception: the double-sided crepe paper (also called *doublette*).

There are really only two points that I consider important when creating paper flowers with crepe paper. One is understanding the fiber direction, and the other is to never leave the paper untouched. Paper has a fiber direction (grain) just as fabric does. The fibers give the material strength, durability, and stretch. This is obvious in crepe paper while it's less noticeable in, for example, silk paper. By following the grain of the paper, you can engage with its characteristics. Do a test where you cut two similar ovals, one along the grain and the other across it. Shape a petal, and then you'll see the difference. You should always keep in the back of your mind to cut along the fibers. When you do that, you'll be able to shape the paper easily, and it will behave just as you expect. If you cut against the grain, you will find it difficult to handle the paper, since it won't follow what your fingers are attempting. (You can read about one exception when I explain how to construct the stem. The arrows shown on the templates indicate the fiber direction.)

If you don't dare to shape a piece of crepe paper using various techniques, you won't experience its capacity and all the possibilities that make it ideal for creating flowers. This trying-out work makes up part of the time you'll need to get a feel for the materials you'll work with.

The feel of the paper and machine lines

Paper is a sensitive material that's affected by sunlight and humidity. Sunlight bleaches paper, and some colors are more sensitive than others. Dampness damages the shape of a finished flower but high humidity does not, as long as you leave the flower untouched. If you're creating a flower when there is high humidity, you will notice that it behaves differently. To dust your flowers, use a hairdryer on low speed and cool air or use compressed air from a can.

The companies I work with have, over the past few years, removed the machine-made lines that had been on crepe paper sized over 100 grams, but you will probably still encounter some. I am talking about the lines that go crossways over the fibers. It is better to work with them than to try to hide them. Keep that in mind when you place your templates.

180-gram crepe paper

A really thick and versatile paper that gives you the freedom to work both with large shapes and small details. This paper is ideal for beginners and was also the first crepe paper I used. It's almost impossible to pull too hard on it or tear it. I would say, though, that it requires you to handle it carefully to get the shape or structure you want. Sometimes you might need to repeat the technique. With certain details, I can let this paper stay unstretched, but never if I use it for petals. In this book, it's most used for details, but in all the projects, wherever double-sided paper is used, you can substitute 180-gram paper. Keep in mind that you can be more forceful in your handling of this paper. Its limit of stretchability is about 260%.

140-gram crepe paper

This paper is similar to the 180-gram paper. For leaves and strips to wrap a stem, I prefer this paper because it's easier to handle and has a softer texture. Also, it has less stretch than the 180-gram paper.

90-gram crepe paper

This paper has a very high amount of stretch, up to 500%, but nevertheless it holds its shape extremely well. I'm very fond of this paper, but it can take awhile to get used to it because of its high amount of stretch. Once you master it, you'll find it gives a feeling of softness that is hard to reach with a coarser paper. In contrast to 180-gram paper, this grade of crepe paper must be handled carefully to understand how much it can be shaped. It doesn't have the same strong structure as heavier paper and so has a special luster and a lighter shine that I like a lot.

60-gram crepe paper

I'd say this paper is the least frequently used by creators who make paper flowers. However, it is a favorite of mine. It's soft and thin and produces a sheer flower, which, in certain basic shades, looks almost transparent. The stretchability is very low, about 140%, so it can take awhile to figure out how the paper behaves. I suggest that you remember to handle this paper lightly. The feeling reminds me a little of a stronger silk paper, but it has a duller surface and yields a more durable flower. This paper is excellent when it comes to dyeing or coloring with dry pastel. I also think it's the best for small details.

Because the paper is thin, you should be very careful when gluing it. Too much glue makes the paper wet and very sensitive. This is the only crepe paper that I sometimes use a glue stick with.

Double-sided crepe paper

Double-sided crepe paper is a 90-gram paper with two thin sheets laminated to each other. The paper is often a different color on each side. It has low stretch, only 90%, and therefore might be experienced as rigid. The paper has a flat structure, which gives a textile-like finish that retains its shape. It's sold in small folded sheets, not rolls, which can be limiting. I count this paper as a type of basic paper, which I often dye/color. If you use a wet dye or dye in larger sheets, leave some of the paper dry. Let it then dry flat so that the two original sheets don't separate from each other.

Cotton balls
Using cotton or wooden balls is an easy way to make your pistils. I use clay, papier-mâché, or highly-degradable paper (facial or toilet tissue or paper towel) for creating round shapes.

Floral tape
When I began making paper flowers, I used floral tape to wrap the stems. Because I find it's limited in colors and difficult to add color to, I switched to working with narrow paper strips. Previously, I was suspicious about what type of glue floral tape contained. Today, I've solved this by using a tape that has the contents clearly listed and is even food-safe. So, I use floral tape in certain cases for pistils or if I'm going to make many tight branchings.

Glue
I personally use a variety of techniques for assembling a flower. Sometimes I have consciously resisted using glue, but that means I need techniques that are most often more time consuming. An alternative to not using glue is to attach only with floral tape, possible only when you use silk paper and crepe paper lower than 60 grams.

The easiest and absolutely the quickest way is to use glue. The glue I recommend is Aleene's Tacky Glue. It's water based and nontoxic; it dries quickly but still allows you enough time to move pieces around a bit.

Glue stick
For crepe paper thinner than 60 grams as well as for silk paper, I sometimes use a glue stick. I notice that other types of glue make the paper too wet.

Hot glue
In principle, I never use hot glue for small and medium-large flowers. If I'm making large, floor flowers, hot glue is often a must. One exception for sometimes using hot glue is when I'm working with an extremely small surface to be glued and want a leaf to lie horizontally without much else to support it.

Steel wire
I use paper with as large an amount of stretchability as possible, but for the framework of the flower itself, I almost always use metal wire. The metal wire constitutes the stem and secures it to the flower. I also use metal wire for details such as pistils and between laminated sheets. A metal wire for the stem is central even for the leaves, which makes it easier to create different structures and to shape them.

You can use both paper-wrapped and plain steel wire. I prefer plain steel wire that I wrap myself because it's cheaper and gives me more control over color and surface. When I construct elements with steel wire—for example, leaves or even for certain petals—I prefer a thin paper-covered steel wire. I use the type of wire that is often used for baking and sugar flowers. The paper surface allows the wire to attach better and minimizes the risk of it sliding out of the leaf.

The steel wire should be straight and not on a roll. For a normal thin flower, I use a wire about 0.047–0.06 in. / American wire gauge 16 or 15 (1.2–1.5 mm) thick and, for leaves, 0.022 in. / 23 gauge (0.55 mm). The wire is usually sized by gauge thickness in the US. The higher the gauge number, the thinner the wire. Straight steel wire is also called elephant wire, stem wire, or floral wire.

Ready-made products

There are a number of manufactured and ready-made pieces for paper flowers, such as pistils, stamens, and other pieces. I never use these types of products because, as much as possible, I want to have control over the materials I use.

Stretching

Cup, bowl

Minimizing fiber visibility

Waves

Shaping with tools

Bending with a dowel

Curling with scissors

Wrinkling/pressing with a dowel

Stretching

When you stretch paper, it becomes thinner and softer, and the fibers show less. The paper becomes easier to shape and cut after stretching. Depending on how much you stretch, the paper will assume different looks and characteristics, and the color will be subdued. Hold the ends of the paper and pull it to stretch. You can also stretch specific sections, such as when cupping for a petal. How much you pull should be a percentage. Use a ruler to control the stretching. Pull, for example, an 8 in. (20 cm) strip to 11¾ in. (30 cm) for 50% stretch. Crepe paper over 100 grams should be stretched for an organic effect.

Cup, bowl

This technique gives the petal a concave, bowl-like shape. Hold the petal between your thumbs and forefingers, move your thumbs to the place you want to cup, then pull your thumbs apart. The edges will remain unshaped. For larger petals, make small, tight pulls.

Minimizing fiber visibility

Another way to decrease the visibility of the fiber is to pull repeatedly in the direction of the fiber bias. Hold the petal in one hand with a tweezer grip and with the other hand pull with your thumb and forefinger. You can even use your nails to enhance the effect.

Waves

This technique gives an organic shape to the top edges of a petal. Hold the outer edge with both hands with a tweezer grip in each and quickly pull them apart from each other, as if to rip the paper without actually tearing it. Make this movement along the entire edge or on parts of the petal. When using paper of a low gram weight, it's best to do this on several petals at the same time.

Shaping with tools

Sometimes, a specific tool is necessary for certain movements or shapes. Consider what you want to achieve—something on hand can work. A ball stylus and dowels are good examples of tools that make shaping easier.

Bending with a dowel

Use varying dimensions of metal dowels, wooden dowels, or strong needles to create bends in the paper. Work in varying directions, both against and with the fiber direction. A narrow tool makes distinctive bends, while a larger tool yields softer shapes.

Curling with scissors

Hold the base of the petal with one hand and lay the scissors with blades closed horizontally on top. Place your thumb over the petal and your forefinger underneath. Pull several times in the fiber direction. Do not change direction, to avoid ripping the petal. If it doesn't feel right, try to curl the paper away from you instead. Lay the scissors, with blades closed, horizontally on the underside of the petal, support it with your forefinger, and pull away from you in a downward direction. Crepe paper of 90 grams or finer should be curled in several layers.

Wrinkling/pressing with a dowel

For more-organic bending, as for a poppy, press the paper together while it stays wrapped around the tool. Then, carefully pull the dowel out and separate the paper without distorting the effect.

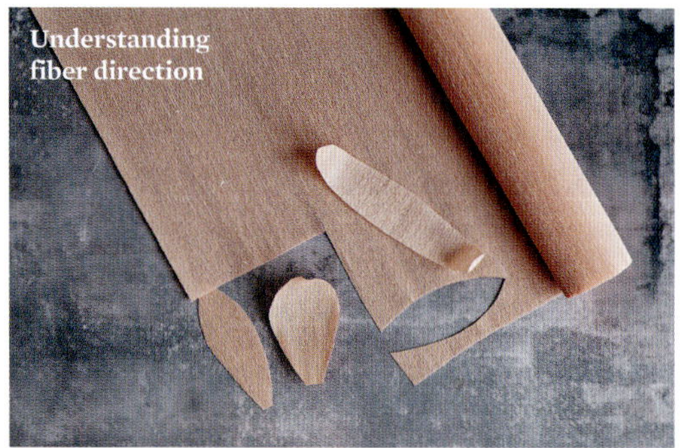
Understanding fiber direction

Strips and measurements

Cutting using a template

Using a weighted template

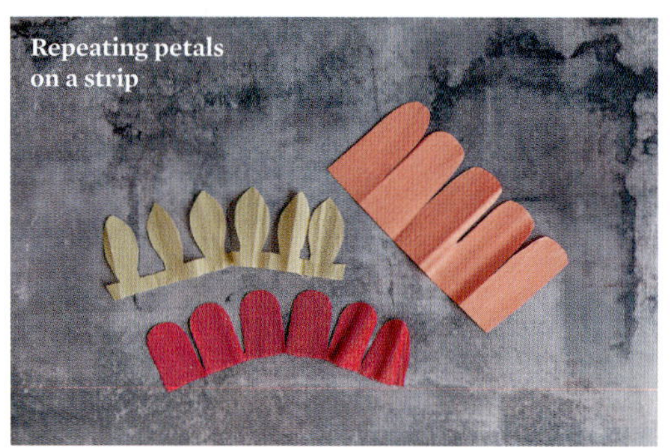
Repeating petals on a strip

Cutting pointed fringe

Cutting out details

Flat folding

Understanding fiber direction

A simple practice: Cut out an oval along the fiber direction (the grain) and another one against it. Cup the ovals with your thumbs and study the differences. Next, take the tips of the ovals and pull them away from each other. One will be rigid and the other stretched out to its maximum.

Strips and measurements

I always begin with strips when I'm making paper flowers. This book gives measurements for each strip, which makes it easier to work with layers, to control measurements and the fiber direction. The length (width) of the strip is given first and then the height. Consider that the height is the measurement that goes in the same direction as the fibers.

Cutting using a template

A template is a guide, but the petal can be scaled up or down to create a variety of sizes. If you change the scale of one part of a flower, it will affect all the other parts. When you cut using a template, follow the fiber direction of the arrow. Cut out several layers at the same time to work effectively: four to five layers for heavier paper and twice as many for thinner paper. Use a clamp to stabilize the template and paper. Cut with long snips and use the strongest point of the scissors at the bottom of the blades. A template can also have a folded edge marked with a dashed line.

Using a weighted template

Cutting with a weighted template can help you maintain the same size on the petals. Cut a weighted template out of strong cardboard, about ¾ in. (2 cm) longer and ⅜ in. (1 cm) wider than your template. Wrap the strip around the template as many times as needed for the correct number of petals. When you pull the template out, the petals will all be the same size as the template. If you need to divide the pile, cut it in manageable layers.

Repeating petals on a strip

Cutting out several petals from a strip with a joined base is an old technique. Fold the strip accordion style so it matches the width of the template. The template shows only a part of the strip, which is seen on the dashed lines showing where the template is folded. Place the base of the template at the bottom of the strip and hold it in place with a clamp. Cut around the template, making sure that the base remains intact.

Freehand cutting and pointed fringe

Cut pointed shapes and details freehand. Use a template as a guide for measurements for shaping. If you want to cut points, such as on a bell or sepal, begin from the outer lines of the template (often a rectangle or square). Then, cut diagonally in from the outer line to the deepest point of the tips.

Cutting out details

To cut details for a petal, use a template as a guide. Cut the petal, following the outer lines on the template. The project instructions will list any details that should be cut before or after shaping. When you cut little details, hold the scissors still and turn the paper instead.

Flat folding

Petals and strips can be made soft or more obvious by folding them, either over the entire surface of the petal or only at the base. Place your thumbs on one end and

Glue

Laminating

Security with a glued ball

Working with a strip on a steel wire

shove the paper against your thumbs with the rest of your fingers. Continue the same way until you reach the opposite end. To strengthen the folds, pull along the fiber direction with one hand while you hold the folded petal with the other hand.

Glue

I most often use a spatula for applying cold glue. When I'm working with thin paper or special techniques, I dab the glue on in small dots to avoid using too much. It's a balancing act: Too much glue makes the paper wet and can cause it to rip so that the pieces do not attach directly. Too little glue doesn't work either. Experiment so you'll know when your paper attaches well and can determine the right amount of glue to use.

Laminating

You can laminate paper to make it thicker or to have two different colors. Press two pieces of paper together with a layer of glue in between. Use a glue stick for thinner paper or tacky glue for thicker paper. Spread the glue evenly with a spatula. For thinner paper, keep it steady; for thicker paper, you can stretch it a little. Glue one surface and lay the other on top, making sure that the fibers on both go in the same direction. Press down well to remove any air bubbles. Work with small areas and use pieces somewhat larger than the template to ensure that the glue covers the entire surface. I often use this technique for fringe. If you laminate fringe, make sure that it dries for at least five minutes before you cut.

Security with a glued ball

One alternative for creating a larger pistil is to glue a ball on a steel wire. Fill the hole in the ball with glue, insert a steel wire, and let it dry completely. Then, apply glue all around and under the ball and cover it with a strip in several layers. The last step is to guarantee that the ball sits very securely, to prevent the pistil and stem from separating from the wire at a later step in the assembly.

Working with a strip on a steel wire

This is a technique I've developed to make it easier and quicker to create flowers that consist of several small flowers, such as, for example, geraniums or delphiniums. I developed this method because I seldom have the patience for this type of flower. I had thought about keeping this method a secret because it took a long time to develop, but, simply put, it is too smart not to share it.

The technique is built on a traditional method but is much more effective for thin paper. Instead of working with many small petals, you'll work with strips joined at the base. Because the paper is the thinnest crepe paper, you can handle many layers at the same time, when you cut, shape, and assemble. With one final press, you can create a whole flower, and once you fully master the technique, it goes lightning fast.

Due to the thinness of the paper, the results are tight without you needing to use small attached surfaces. Additionally, you need only a minimal amount of glue because the damp glue penetrates through all the layers of thin paper. The technique is suitable for every flower, but here is the basic description: Work with one or more strips. Fold the strip lengthwise and then in a pile to cut

Cutting fringe

Making the fringe thinner

Twisting fringe

Using a hook for security

several layers simultaneously. Cut the petals, following the template, leaving the base intact. Divide the strip, following the measurements for the project, and separate the pieces. Dab a few dots of glue onto the fold. If you are using several layers of strips, lay them on each other. Place the paper-covered steel wire in the fold and fold the strip over the wire. Hold the wire with one hand and press the strip against it with the other hand at the same time as you tightly fold the strip together. When you are finishing folding, fold the wire down so it becomes a stem.

Cutting fringe

Cutting fringe is useful both for stamens and pistils, no matter whether they are small and detailed or large and luxuriant. By mastering this technique, you'll find endless possibilities. The thinner the fringe you can cut, the finer level of detail you can accomplish. Use strips in various lengths and heights. It is common to combine different types of fringe with a variety of looks in the same flower.
It is important to follow the given measurements for each fringe because deviations can significantly change the look. To cut long fringe, fold the strip several times so you can cut several layers simultaneously. If it is difficult to hold the strip steady, use a metal clamp at the base and rest your hand with the clamp on a table. This stability makes it easier to cut fine fringe. I most often use scissors with long blades, up to 3¼–4 in. (8–10 cm). The reason for this is that I prefer to make just one cut per snip. Many prefer precision scissors, so experiment to see what works for you. The basic rule for fringe is that the entire base of the strip is the surface that will be glued firmly to the rest of the flower while the fringes remain unglued.

Making the fringe thinner

One technique for refining your fringe is to gather the cut strips between your palms. Do not roll the strips, but collect them in one pile. Press your palms together and move your upper hand back and forth so the fringe twists. Repeat the process until you are satisfied with the result. If you are working with a laminated, wet fringe, you should avoid this technique because the paper layers can easily separate from each other.

Twisting fringe

Twisting one fringe at a time takes time, and I most often use this method for pistils with fewer stamens. The technique is particularly good for small, detailed parts where precision is important. By twisting each fringe separately, you'll have far more control and can create a more detailed result on the pistils, which won't be too big or complicated.

Using a hook for security

When you are wrapping fringe around the wire, begin by making a tight hook in one end of the wire and catch the fringe in it. It's important not to stretch the fringe at the same time as you wrap, unless the instructions suggest otherwise. If the fringe rips while you wrap, begin again at the same place where it separated.

It is important to press the fringe against the stem with your free hand at the same time as you wrap, to ensure that it sits on very firmly. Also take care to keep the fringe at the same level as you wrap, or it will slide. It makes a big difference in the final look if the fringe is wrapped along the stem or is held at a constant point.

Adding structure to your flowers

There are many creative ways to add structure to pistils and stamens, ways that give the flowers a realistic feeling of pollen and liveliness. The possibilities are endless for adding more details and depth to your flowers. Although there are many synthetic materials on the market, I prefer using natural alternatives. You can, for example, gather materials directly from the garden.

One problem with dried plants is that they often fall apart over time or even as you work with them. To counteract this, you can spray them with hairspray or lacquer. Personally, I don't care for this method, and so I avoid dried plants. If you choose to use dye, that's often sufficient to hold the material together.

You can even experiment with turmeric, polenta, or pepper, but my best tip is semolina. I got the tip about semolina from a visitor to my exhibit at the Sven-Harry Art Museum. She said that her older relatives used semolina for creating similar details on their paper flowers in Poland in the 1930s. I grind the semolina finely and blend it with natural pigments to obtain the desired color and texture.

Regardless of what material you use, the easiest way to get it to attach is to apply it sparingly with glue on the surfaces where you want to make an effect. Dab or add the glue with a spatula.

Leaves

Making leaves is time consuming, and I would be lying if I said that I love it. However, leaves are important for finishing the flowers. An arrangement with leaves adds a dynamic look and depth to the bouquet. It grounds it. The fact is that you'll need more leaves than you might believe. They function the same way as the background in a painting does. The greenery, no matter what shade, contributes to showcasing the flowers more distinctly.

When I make an arrangement of several flowers, I always make sure to increase the shades of green and add stems with only leaves on them in various shapes, colors, and sizes. This creates a more lifelike and interesting bouquet.

The easiest way is to make leaves without any wire. In some cases, it's enough to simply free-cut oval shapes in the fiber direction and attach them on the stem. But I recommend that you master a basic technique where each leaf consists of two halves. This is useful and makes it possible to create all the leaves shown in this book.

When creating leaves, scale the templates up and down for various sizes. An individual flower often consists of several leaves, and making them in several sizes creates dynamism. One leaf's template with asymmetrical sides can even be paired with a symmetrical leaf. Let creativity be your guide.

The technique relies on the fibers meeting diagonally at a straight centerline, which makes the nerve at the center of the leaf. The fibers point 45 degrees in upward and outward directions. In order to be able to bend the leaf, it is advantageous to insert a fine wire into the leaf. The wire will be hidden in a fold. By working with and following the fibers and their characteristics together with the wire, you'll get endless possibilities for creating realistic leaves. Even small details function noticeably better in combination with the fiber direction.

You can stretch 100–180-gram crepe paper about 75%–100% before you use it. If you use thinner paper, you can leave it unstretched; likewise if you use double-sided. I often laminate the paper I use for leaves because that gives them extra strength, particularly for larger leaves; I always laminate before I cut out the leaves.

If you are using double-sided, or another paper with different colors, you must cut two pieces for each leaf to have the same color on both sides. Turn one piece so that the sides with the same color lie against each other before you cut diagonally.

In reality, leaves often consist of various nuances and colors, not just green. Also, green is a color that generally fades more quickly than other colors. So, it's both creative and advantageous to intensify the green color with some of the techniques described in the section on dyeing (page 44).

The most suitable wire to use in leaf making is paper-covered steel wire, 24 gauge (0.51 mm).

1.

2.

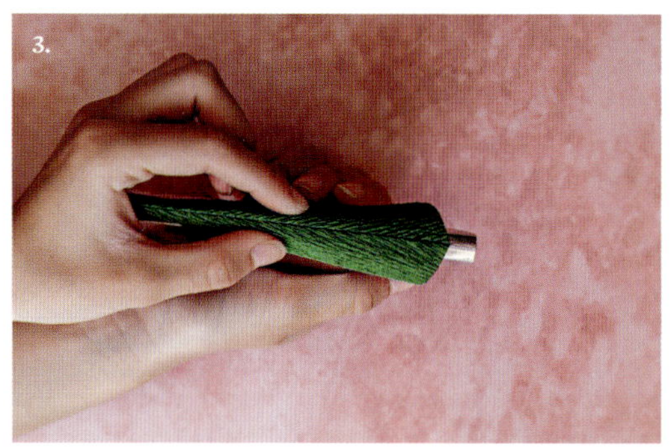
3.

4.

5.

Branching

Basic techniques for leaf making

Cut a rectangle or square somewhat larger than your template. Divide the paper by cutting it diagonally. To make it easier, scratch it diagonally with a ruler and deepen it with the back of a knife. Turn one part so that the fibers meet (photo **1**).

Lay the triangles on top of each other, with the fibers in an upward direction. Apply a thin line of glue along one triangle's longest side (a maximum of 1⁄16 in. [2 mm] wide, thinner for smaller leaves). Pinch over the glued surface several times to ensure that it has attached properly. Add a clamp along the long side where the glue ends (photo **2**).

Hold the leaf securely with a clamp and then open the leaf on the topside. Let the clamp remain, to form a sharp line when you fold both sides down, toward the clamp. This clear fold will make it easier for when you later include the wire. Let the piece dry for a while and then remove the clamp (photo **3**).

Fold the leaf so that the "hem" is on the back. Round the corners on the back of the hem with scissors. Lay a thin line of glue in the inner fold; it doesn't matter which side you choose. Place a paper-covered wire in the glue, about 3⁄8 in. (1 cm) from the top, and fold it over the hem. Press well so everything adheres (photo **4**).

The basic instructions for green leaves are complete. Cut, following your choice of template, and shade the leaf as you desire (photo **5**).

Branching

Certain flowers, such as the rose in this book, have several small leaves that together build a larger leaf. The same basic technique is used for longer stems, covered with small flowers. The principle is to join a smaller stem with a main stem at one point and twist it in under the strip so that it sits tightly to the main stem.

One example is the rose twig, which can consist of three, five, or seven smaller leaves. Begin with a single leaf and bend the rest of the leaves at a 45-degree angle out from the stem, to make it easier to attach them when you wrap them at the base of the main stem with paper strips or floral tape. Follow the instructions for spacing between the leaves. When you've wrapped the leaves in by about 3⁄8 in. (1 cm), trim them to prevent the main stem from becoming too thick. Attach the main stem at the flower stem, following the same principle.

Covering with a strip

Quick technique for short stems

Tightening up the stem

Sepals on a strip

The flower stem

You can buy paper-covered steel wire, but you should master doing the covering yourself to create dynamism, gain artistic freedom, and be able to make flowers and leaves with several parts. When you finish the stems with strips, even the underside of the flower is whole and complete. You can wrap wire both with paper strips and floral tape. Floral tape is used by florists, but I seldom use it for stems because of the limited color choices and the difficulty of coloring it. Floral tape can still be useful for making pistils. Whether you use paper strips or floral tape, the technique is the same. When you wrap floral tape, no glue is necessary because the tape becomes sticky and attaches as you stretch it while wrapping. The stretching activates the tape's glue.

Covering with a strip

Cut strips from 90–180-gram crepe paper, ¼–⅜ in. (0.5–1 cm) wide. Cut against the fibers and stretch the strip out before you begin wrapping. Attach the strip to the wire with a bit of glue. Hold the strip diagonally and wrap it with a two-handed grip: One hand holds the stretched strip while the other wraps the stem. Wrap the entire wire and apply a little glue now and then. The glue can be applied to the stem or the strip, but it's important to add it successively. If the strip breaks or ends, begin again from the same point with a new strip. When you have finished, tear the strip and fold it in. For a stronger stem, repeat with several layers.

Quick technique for short stems

When I developed techniques to make work on small and multiple flowers more effective, I used the same principles as for the stems. By working with thin crepe paper and a little pressure, you can quickly wrap short and thin stems. Begin with strips and the templates for the respective project. The template even includes a free-cut section for the sepal leaves. Apply a little glue along the wire, press the paper firmly around the wire, and let the sepals drop precisely under the flower.

Tightening up the stem

Roll the stem between your palms or fingertips with an even pressure to ensure that the paper attaches thoroughly and that everything is tight and evenly spaced along the entire stem. This technique can always be used on stems.

Sepals on a strip

If your project includes sepals from a strip, it is important to always bend the tips out over a dowel, no matter the size and length. The bend should be directed away from the petals. Attach the strips on top where the petals meet the stem. Sometimes it can be necessary to fold the strip while you glue it around the stem for a tighter base. Lightly press the bottom of the strip together while you wrap and attach with glue. If the bottom is wide, for example, due to a large pistil or many petals, you can shape the strip into a cylinder and use a dowel as a support as you glue. This is similar to the technique for making a bell. Move the cylinder from the top and down onto the stem.

Dyeing

This book focuses on techniques and the anatomy of flowers, which I consider to be the basics of the handcraft. The next step is working with dyeing, shading, and other details. I give tips on the details for certain projects, but with this aspect, you'll come closer to making your own personal expressions, and so I don't want to steer your choices. You can use all the available construction materials, those you prefer to work with. Just as in nature, there are many nuances and details. In the same way, you can work with color on your own flowers. Study nature and see what happens over a season, and transfer that to your paper flowers.

One important rule to remember is that wet dye breaks down the paper's fibers. Although the paper can be revived and the fibers can repair themselves to a certain extent, the crepe-paper structure is changed. For that reason, for dyeing, you should dampen the paper before you cut the leaves and petals, and the paper must be completely dry before you work with it. Here are a few tips on the different dyeing techniques I use:

Using crepe paper's own pigment

One way to dye a larger amount of paper is to work with strips suitable to the height of the template. Roll the paper out and then back loosely. Heat the water to boiling point and make a dye bath with either liquid watercolors or bits of waste crepe paper. The heavier papers in strong colors contain a lot of pigment. If you have several containers, you can dip the roll into several shades, one after the other. Note that the paper absorbs water quickly, so you must work carefully. Avoid overwetting the paper and make sure that some of it stays dry, which works as a reinforcement to prevent the paper from disintegrating.

Dry pastels
You can easily work with a variety of shades and create soft, natural color transitions. Dry pastels are used in a dry state. Pan pastel lies in a cup, so you can paint directly from the cup. It has a high amount of color pigment, which means that you need to add only a very small amount to get results. The composition of pan pastels means that it feels almost greasy when applying, which helps it adhere. The color is also lightfast, so it won't fade over time.

Oil pastel chalk
You can also work with oil pastel chalk. The oily, covering consistency produces an immediate effect, so begin carefully. You can, for example, even use this medium by transferring the dye to a sponge and then pressing with the sponge on the paper.

Markers
It's easy to use markers for small details. However, when you use a marker type such as Copic, you need to keep in mind that a wet marker affects the paper the same way that a wet dye does. You can benefit from this and create fine transitions. For anyone not familiar with working with brushes, a pen such as Copic can be a good way to begin. For example, Posca, which is a completely covering marker with high pigmentation, does not at all spread in the same way on paper, which can be a positive. The negative aspect is that it's difficult to produce natural shifts.

Coffee and tea
Coffee and tea make pretty and natural dyes. I personally think that coffee has too strong of a scent, so I use it only for very small details. Tea produces a perfect subtle off-white tone, which is useful for lots of things. Brew about eight tea bags in four cups of boiling water. Let the tea steep for about ten minutes, so the color deepens, and then let it cool completely before you use it. Use a large brush to apply the tea on white crepe paper. Hang the paper up or lay it on a protected surface to dry. If possible, dry the paper outside on a warm day to speed up the process. The drying time can be longer inside, sometimes overnight.

The Flowers

Anemone

With its dark and distinct pistils, the anemone lends extra depth to an arrangement. I personally think that the black color is important even when the rest of the bouquet is light and colorful. Black adds a sharp contrast as well as taking away a little of the romantic feeling. Anemones can have both larger and smaller pistils, so experiment with the size while also considering that even the stamens might need to be longer. Even a single flower can have different color transitions. Work with dry pastel or dyeing on the paper (see the section on page 45).

The pattern has a total of ten petals per flower, but, at the same time, I love to make anemones a little skewed, so it's important not to lose balance. Always cut a few extra petals and feel free to give each flower an individual shape.

Materials

white crepe paper (#600) 180 g/m^2
black crepe paper (#602) 180 g/m^2
blue crepe paper (#394) 90 g/m^2
green crepe paper (#962) 140 g/m^2
highly-degradable paper (facial or toilet tissue or paper towel)
paper-covered steel wire, 17 gauge (1.4 mm)
black pen
cold glue such as tacky glue

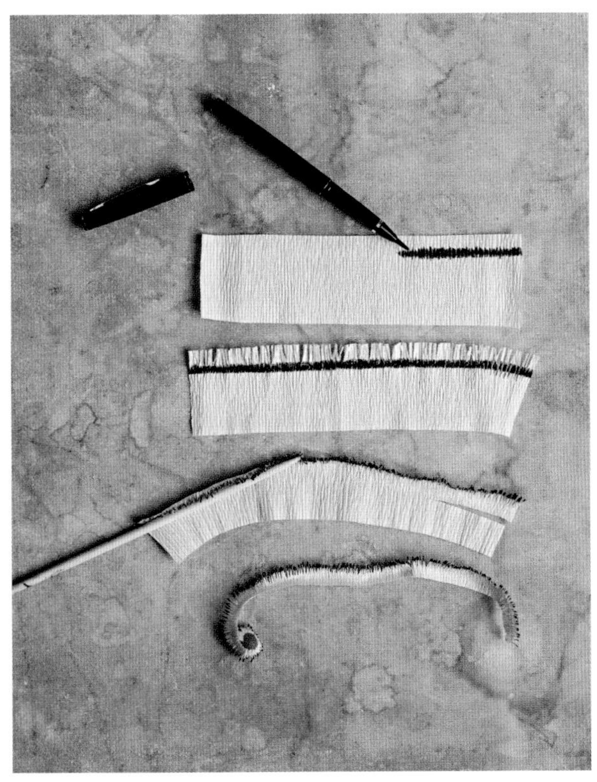

Stamens

Cut 1 strip of white crepe paper, 4 × 2 in. (10 × 5 cm). Stretch the strip out completely. With a black pen, draw a straight horizontal line ⅜ in. (1 cm) down from the top of the strip. The line should be about ¼ in. (5 mm) wide. Repeat on the opposite side of the strip. Here, you can decide if you want to use a thicker color for more-obvious pistils, but then be sure to include extra drying time.

Cut a fine fringe, with a depth of about 1⁄16 in. (2 mm) below the line. Trim the top of the strip to the center of the black line. Gather the strip and roll it between your palms to finesse the fringe (see page 35).

Lay a dowel where the fringe ends, and fold the entire strip over the dowel. Trim the length again, but now on the lower edge, so a base of ¼ in. (5 mm) remains.

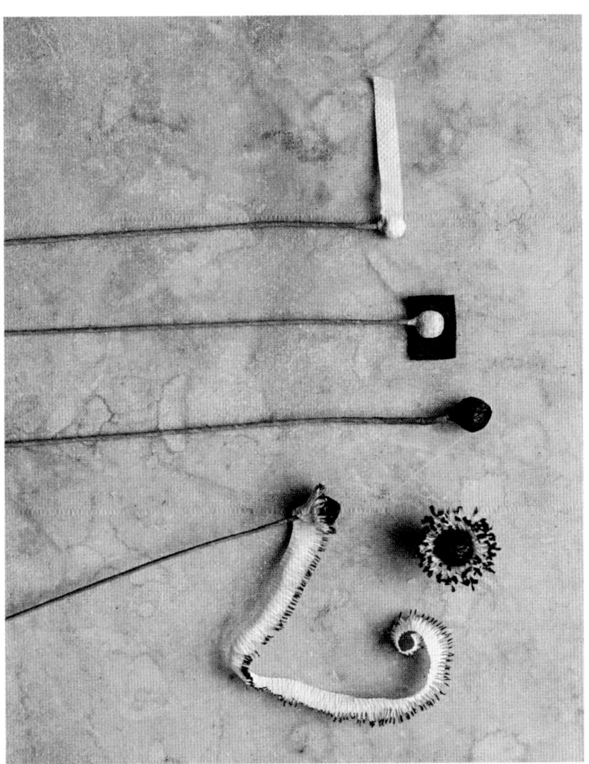

Pistils

Begin with the paper-covered wire. Peel away about ¾ in. (2 cm) of the paper at the top and shape a small hook. Wrap the highly-degradable paper with glue around the wire to create a round shape with a diameter of approximately ⅜ in. (1 cm). Cut out a bit
of black crepe paper about 1 × ⅝ in. (2.5 × 1.5 cm). Apply glue on the paper ball and place the black paper around it. Use your fingers for shaping so that the crepe paper is tightly wrapped around the ball, and, as necessary, trim away any excess on the underside.

Attach the strip with glue under the ball. Place the strip so the folded part lifts the strip away from the ball.

Petals and assembly

Cut a strip of blue crepe paper 9¾ × 2⅜ in. (25 × 6 cm). Stretch it out to 11¾ in. (30 cm). Cut out the petals, following the template on page 142. You'll need 5 petals each of the smaller and larger sizes. I always cut out a few extra petals to use if I need to adjust the balance on the flower.

Shape the flower by pulling scissors along the fiber direction. Lightly press on the top part of the petal to create a cupped shape. Finally, fold the lower part of the petal over a dowel.

Attach the smaller petals around the pistils. Continue with the larger petals on the next layer, placing them below the intersecting points of petals on the first layer. Make sure that the balance of the flower is good, by looking at it from above. Add extra petals if necessary.

Leaves and a strip for the stem

Wrap the stem, using a green strip cut against the grain. Begin directly underneath the petals and wrap the entire stem.

Cut 1 strip of green crepe paper, 4 × 2¾ in. (10 × 7 cm). Stretch it out and cut out the leaves, following the template on page 142. Twist the points on the leaves. Then, twist the entire leaf in one direction. Unfold the leaf without distorting the effect. Pinch the lower part of the leaf together and attach it near the top of the stem. Each flower should have at least 2 leaves, but preferably more.

Icelandic Poppy

The poppy is the first flower I created when I began working with crepe paper. It is perhaps not so strange that I have become a little tired of it over time. On the other hand, it's a flower that really lends itself to being made with crepe paper, which is perfect for the organically shaped petals with soft, billowing lines. It's a simple flower to make, but it can also be very advanced, with a plethora of details and nuances. A flower to grow with, so to speak.

For example, the pistils can, in principle, be changed as much as you like. Here, I show how you use highly-degradable paper as well as wrapping with floral tape. Together, they have a consistency almost like clay. Use tools such as a metal dowel to shape it. You'll see that this bit is very satisfying. At an exhibition I contributed to, a woman said that in her homeland of Poland, semolina was often used for details such as stamens. I grind the semolina and then add pigment from the art shop.

Materials

yellow crepe paper (#578) 180 g/m^2
green crepe paper (#558) 180 g/m^2
powder-dyed crepe paper (#358) 90 g/m^2
double-sided crepe paper
highly-degradable paper (facial or toilet tissue or paper towel)
paper-covered steel wire, 17 gauge (1.4 mm)
floral tape, green and yellow
strong thread
semolina and pigment for structure
cold glue such as tacky glue

Pistils

Bend the wire into an eye loop. Tear 1 strip of highly-degradable paper (paper towel, for example). Use the cold glue to attach the paper around the wire loop and shape it into an oval ball, following the template on page 143.

Wrap green floral tape around the paper, making several layers until the pistil feels smooth and even. Shape by pressing with your fingers.

Divide the yellow tape lengthwise and twist it into a thread about 13¾ in. (35 cm) long. Wrap the twisted thread around the ball to create a cross pattern. Begin with a few wraps at the base, letting the thread wind diagonally over the ball, and then twist it a half turn around the ball. Repeat this sequence four times, changing direction on every new turn. Resist glueing during this step. End by winding the strong thread to secure the tape and then knot.

Use 6–8 in. (15–20 cm) of the green tape to wrap from the bottom of the ball to the middle, repeating until the surface feels even. Use a metal dowel to shape and adjust the ball as necessary.

For a uniform color and further development of the details, you can also wrap the pistil with a thinner paper such as 60-gram paper. Attach with a little glue and then shape the pistil. The previous steps have made the pistil a basic form to proceed from.

Stamen

Cut 2 strips of yellow and green crepe paper 2¾ × 2 in. (7 × 5 cm). Stretch the strips out as far as they will go. Laminate the strips, using glue (see page 33). Press the strips together and even out the edges as necessary. Apply a thin layer of glue along the top edge of the strip and fold down ¼ in. (0.5 cm). Repeat the folding once more. Press it together very firmly. Let the strip dry for about 10 minutes. It is important that the paper remain slightly damp, so that the strip will be easier to shape later on.

When you cut the fringe in damp paper, avoid twisting it between your palms to make it thinner. There is a risk that the laminated sheets will separate. Try to cut as fine a fringe as possible, leaving a base about ¼ in. (0.5 cm).

Shaping

Shape the fringe while it is still damp. An S shape is important so that the fringe will be tightly wound around the pistil during assembly. At the same time it should have a cup shape where the fringe leaves off. Use a heavy, round needle or dowel to make the S shape, following the photo. The fringe forms the concave part, which will be the visible part if you look at the flower from above. The entire part of the strip is thus convex. This is the part you glue firmly below the pistil in the next step.

Assembly

Attach the stamens around the pistil with cold glue and avoid placing them too high up on the ball. For the best balance, I recommend that you place the stamens from the edge underneath the rounding and up to where the tape ends. Placement outside this surface can lead to an unbalanced end product. It is very important to press the strip very firmly against the pistil at the same time as wrapping it around the stem.

Structure

Glue the tops of the stamens, preferably using a spatula to dab the glue farthest out. Then roll the pistil in a bowl of semolina so the grain adheres to the glue. Let it all dry completely before you attach the petals.

Petals

Cut a strip of crepe paper 19¾ × 4¾ in. (50 × 12 cm). Stretch the strip out completely. Fold the strip into a pile with 4 layers and then fold it at the center to make an open and a closed side with a folded edge. Cut out the leaves, following the template on page 143.

To shape the petals, fold them by pushing each petal between your fingers, following the technique for flat folding (see page 31). Twist the petals for an organic shape. Twist along the fiber grain, first in one direction and then in the other, such as when you wring out a rag. Carefully press down on the top to further soften the fibers.

Carefully pry the base up. Apply cold glue on the lower surface, about ⅜ in. (1 cm) up the petal, and then press well so that the petal forms a fan. Pinch the base and press with your thumb on the opposite hand so the petal bends backward. Remove any excess by trimming away the corner of the lower edge so the end forms a point.

Attaching the petals

Attach 2 petals directly below the pistil, opposite each other, where the strip for the stem begins. Place another 2 petals between the remaining 2 to fill out the flower form.

Cover the base of the petals with 1 extra strip of crepe paper. Glue well at the base and shape by wrapping the strip a few times. Continue down along the stem as needed.

Final shaping

Shape the petals by carefully prying them up without losing their organic form. Work with the technique of wrinkling/pressing with a dowel (see page 29). Use both wider and narrower dowels and twist the petal in various directions.

Leaves and creating the buds

Make the leaves, following the basic instructions and using the templates on page 143.

For the sepals on the buds, cut 2 pieces of double-sided crepe paper, about 4 × 1¼ in. (10 × 3 cm). Round off both ends. Twist every piece at the center a half turn. Place your thumb on one half and press it into the other half of the paper. Repeat with both pieces.

Gather the paper you will use for your petals and cut out 2 smaller leaves, shaping them organically. Attach them on a wire. Attach both green parts of the buds on each side of the flower petals. Then, wrap the stem with the paper strip.

English Bluebells

Most people think that making a bluebell from paper is complicated, when, actually, it's exactly the opposite. It's easy to make several of them while you're at it, then fill a whole stem with them. Arranging a row of the same type of flower in a bouquet is something that breaks the form and therefore produces a playful effect. In this pattern, I cut the bell tips freehand is because it is clearly easier. If you are uncertain about how to guide the scissors, first practice on a smooth paper and see what happens.

Materials

blue crepe paper (#394) 90 g/m^2
pale-yellow crepe paper (#577) 180 g/m^2
light-green crepe paper (#365) 90 g/m^2
green crepe paper (#368) 90 g/m^2
paper-covered steel wire, 23 and 21 gauge (0.55 and 0.7 mm)
round dowel, ⅜ in. (1 cm) in diameter
tool with a ball, ⅜ in. (1 cm) in diameter
cold glue such as tacky glue

The bells

Cut a narrow piece of blue crepe paper, 1 × 19¾ in. (2.5 × 50 cm). Cut in the same direction as the fiber grain. Use a dowel to shape the paper into a tube by stretching it and overlapping the edges by ¼ in. (5 mm). Glue along the long side, pressing well along the join, and then let it dry.

Cut the tube into 10 pieces, 2 in. (5 cm) long. Cut one end on each piece into 17 very narrow tips, ⅝ in. (1.5 cm) deep, following the template on page 144. Bend the tips around a thin metal dowel. Press the ball stylus through the top opening and pinch it on the lower edge of the ball so it forms a rounded bottom.

The pistils

Cut 1 pale-yellow paper strip, 4 × 2⅜ in. (10 × 6 cm). Stretch the strip out as much as possible and divide it into 2 pieces. Cover one strip with cold glue and laminate both pieces together. Apply a thin layer of glue at the top of the strip and fold the top edge down about 1⁄16 in. (2 mm). Fold it down once more so you have a total of 6 layers on the top edge. Press everything together firmly. Let the strip dry for about 10 minutes.

Cut a thin fringe with a depth of 1⅜ in. (3.5 cm). Divide these up into small groups of 3 fringes each. Carefully bend the tops outward, using a metal dowel.

Divide the 23-gauge (0.55 mm) wire into pieces 4 in. (10 cm) long. Make a hook at the top of the wire and press it tightly against the pistil and then glue it. Repeat this step with all the pieces.

Joining the bells and pistils

Take the blue paper you used for the bells and cut 1 piece 2 × 1¼ in. (5 × 3 cm). Stretch it out lightly. Cut out 10–15 small leaves, following the template on page 144. Use the scissors to pull them along the grain. Cut a strip of the blue paper, ⅜ in. (1 cm) wide.

Insert the wire into a bell. Pinch the bell and pistil base together and fasten with glue. Twist the strip over the base of the bell, continuing 1¼ in. (3 cm) down the wire. Finally, attach the blue leaves with a spot of glue. Repeat for all the bells.

Attaching the bells to the stem

Take the paper-covered 23-gauge (0.55 mm) wire. Cut 1 light-green strip with the fiber grain, ¼ in. (5 mm) wide. Stretch the strip out by 50% and wrap it the same way as for wrapping a stem, while also attaching the bells.

Begin by first laying the bells by the wire for the stem. At the same level as for the blue leaves, begin wrapping the green strip and joining the bells to the stem. Space the bells about 1¼ in. (3 cm) apart. The flower stems align with the main stem and are covered with the green strip. Repeat until you have attached 10 bluebells on the stem.

The flowers should point upward, all in the same direction. Bend each bell so it softly swings forward.

Green leaves

Prepare pieces of green crepe paper #365 and #368 with a measurement of 6 × 8 in. (15 × 20 cm). Make 3–5 leaves of varying sizes. Lightly stretch the papers and divide them into 3–5 pieces of each color. Apply glue to the pieces and place the wires, centered, ¾ in. (2 cm) from the top edge. Lay the remaining pieces on top of the wire and press firmly. Cut, following the template on page 144, and pinch each leaf together. Cut a strip ⅜ in. (1 cm) wide against the grain. Gather the leaves and attach them with the strip like a tuft at the base of the main stem.

Water Lily

Actually, it was the leaves I was after. Something big with a whole surface to play with. Then, the flowers followed, of course. A water lily has a fairy-tale element to it. The best thing about paper flowers here is that a water lily can become a cut flower, which, in a way, seems obvious in a bouquet.

Materials

yellow crepe paper (#576) 180 g/m^2
white double-sided crepe paper
green crepe paper
green double-sided crepe paper
green silk paper, 11¾ × 11¾ in. (30 × 30 cm)
steel wire, 17 gauge (1.4 mm)
paper-covered steel wire, 24 gauge (0.51 mm)
cold glue such as tacky glue

Pistils

Cut 1 strip of yellow crepe paper measuring 17¾ × 2⅜ in. (45 × 6 cm). Fold the strip down the center and laminate it with cold glue, making sure that the glue evenly covers the entire surface. Divide the strip into 3 pieces: 1 that is 8 × 1¼ in. (20 × 3 cm) and 2 smaller pieces adjusted in height along the lower edge: 1 strip measuring 4 × ⅝ in. (10 × 1.5 cm) as well as 1 that is 6 × ¾ in. (15 × 2 cm).

Cut fringe on the shortest strip, with a depth of ⅜ in. (1 cm). Let it dry for about 5 minutes. Rub it between your palms to finesse the fringe (see page 35).

Cut fringe on the other short strip, with a depth of ⅝ in. (1.5 cm). Twist the fringe and bend it over a dowel.

Cut 1 in. deep (2.5 cm) fringe on the longest strip. The width of the fringe should be about ¼ in. (5 mm). Cut the top into points, following the template on page 144. Twist the top of each fringe. Fold the twisted pieces of the strip over a dowel, directed away from the center point.

Shape a tight hook on one end of a piece of wire and hang it on the fringe of the shortest strip. Attach all 3 strips, one after the other onto the hook, keeping them at the same level on their bottom edges.

Petals

Cut the petals from the white double-sided crepe paper, following the template on page 144, making a total of 10 petals of each size.

Lightly cup each petal at the top and slightly bend each inward by drawing your thumb and forefinger in one movement in that direction.

Attaching the petals and a thicker stem

Attach the petals below the pistil. The surface for attachment is relatively small, and your goal is a relatively flat shape for the lower part of the water lily. Begin with 5 small petals for the first layer and continue with the remaining 5 of the same size, attaching them in between petals on the first set. Continue the same way with the 10 medium-size petals and end with the 10 largest. Make sure that the flower is balanced in shape. Let the innermost petals, those nearest the pistil, poke up, and the outer petals lie more horizontally.

Cut 4 sepals from the green double-sided crepe paper, following the template on page 144.

Cup them and attach them in doubled pairs to each other.

To make a thicker stem, wrap the original one with some highly-degradable paper and glue. Finally, use 1 strip, cut against the grain, the same color as the sepals.

Leaves

Gather 5–7 paper-covered wires in a bundle to make a stem for the leaf. Wrap a paper strip beginning 4 in. (10 cm) from one end, around the wire bundle, using glue.

Fold out the other parts of the wires. Take 5 sheets of silk paper measuring 11¾ × 11¾ in. (30 × 30 cm). Cut a notch of about 4 in. (10 cm) along the grain on all of them.

Glue the surface of the first silk paper and set the stem on the paper, then continue by wrapping glue and silk paper. The last sheet will be the back of the leaf; turn the finished leaf and let dry. Cut out the leaf shape, following the template on page 145. Join the flower and leaf.

Sweet Pea

Sometimes you need quick flowers, those you can make a lot of in a short time and, in that way, fill out a bouquet. In that case, you prioritize the overall visual effect rather than the details. Sweet peas are excellent for this. They can be simplified without losing their graceful feeling and, at the same time, contribute with their ever-so-important green leaves. For several workshops, I taught a quick variation, but this pattern is for a somewhat more detailed sweet pea. You can make it even more advanced if you add buds and coloration.

Most of all, you can make it more quickly by skipping the pistils. Follow the instructions for the petals and green leaves. Use two paper-covered wires, 17 gauge (1.4 mm). Glue the petals on top of one wire and on each end of the other. Lay the wires tightly against each other and hold them with pliers at a suitable branching point. Wrap the wire with two flowers, first to the right and then to the left, and press together with the pliers until they are stable. Glue the branching and wrap the green leaf around the knot. Finally, bend the stems into an organic shape.

Materials

cream-colored crepe paper (#352) 90 g/m^2
blue crepe paper (#381) 90 g/m^2
green crepe paper (#377) 90 g/m^2
paper-covered steel wire, 23 and 17 gauge (0.55 and 1.4 mm)
cold glue such as tacky glue

Pistil

Cut 1 strip of cream-colored crepe paper against the grain, ⅜ × 11¾ in. (1 × 30 cm).

Cut 4 in. (10 cm) lengths of the thinner wire. Shape a drop at one end of the wire. Wrap the strip together with glue around the drops. At the same time, stretch the strip as you wrap. Pinch it flat with your fingers or pliers.

From 1 strip of the same paper, cut pieces ¾ in. (2 cm) long, following the template on page 142. Pull this backward over the scissors. To add a backward shape to the ovals, draw them over the blade of the scissors. Then, firmly pinch an oval on each drop, using glue, and attach the back part of the drop, as shown in the photo.

Petals

Cut 1 strip from the blue crepe paper, 8 × 4 in. (20 × 10 cm). Cut, following the template on page 142, and prepare at least 3 flowers. You'll need 3 larger petals and 6 smaller ones.

Take 3 petals at a time. Hold them firmly on the lower section of the petal and pull out along the grain with the blade of the scissors. Pull 5–6 times per pile, until the petals feel stiff.

Shaping the petals

Continue working with 3 petals at a time.

Create a wavy shape along the top edge, using the wave-shaping technique (see page 29). Bend the smaller petals at the top edge with a dowel. Make two bends per petal, each in the opposite direction. You can also use the wrinkle/press technique with a dowel for curlier petals (see page 29).

Separate the larger petals from each other.

Folding the larger petals

Now you can work with one petal at a time. Make a sharp fold, centered vertically on the larger petal. Apply a little glue, using a pin. This way, you will make a permanent fold. Pinch the base together and bend the lower edge by placing it over the thinner dowel.

Joining the petals and stem

Use 2 smaller petals and 1 larger one per flower. Begin with the smaller petals, pinching them together at the base and attaching them behind the pistil. Center the larger petal behind the smaller ones and bend it outward with your thumb at the base. Cut a piece of green crepe paper, 2 × 2 in. (5 × 5 cm), stretch it out to the maximum, and cut it, following the template on page 142. Bend the tips outward with a dowel. Press the strip around the stem, using glue. Roll the stem between your palms to tighten it. Bend each flower forward. Cut 1 narrow strip along the grain, ⅜ in. (1 cm), of stretched green crepe paper. Attach the individual flowers onto the paper-covered wire (17 gauge [1.4 mm]), working from the top down.

Leaves

With the stretched green crepe paper, make 2 leaves, following the instructions and template on page 142. Attach the leaves on each end of a wire, 23 gauge (0.55 mm), and fold the wire double so that both leaves point in the same direction. Cut 1 strip of stretched green crepe paper along the grain, ¾ × 4 in. (2 × 10 cm). Make a fold at the center along the grain, apply glue, and lay flat. Place one double-folded wire with the leaves with another double-folded wire, 23 gauge (0.55 mm), in the glue and press the paper together. Twist the stem to create structure, then work the paper so the stem is flat. Turn the 2 ends of the wire sticking up over the stem around a metal dowel to make spirals. Attach and wrap the leaves around the stem. Cut small oval leaves and attach them on the stem to hide the branching.

Peony

Over the past few years, I've begun to like simple peonies more and more, at least when it comes to paper flowers. Perhaps I have too little patience for flowers with a lot of petals. This peony can be worked with the same process, no matter whether you let the resulting flower be more or less full bloom. An extremely blossomed peony of this type is, for me, at its most beautiful stage, just before the petals fall to the ground.

Materials

pink crepe paper (#212) 60 g/m^2
light-green crepe paper (#566) 180 g/m^2
yellow crepe paper (#17ES) 180 g/m^2
pale-yellow crepe paper (#280) 60 g/m^2
white double-sided crepe paper, here, dyed with pink and green watercolors
paper-covered steel wire, 23 and 15 gauge (0.55 and 1.5 mm)
cold glue such as tacky glue

Pistils

Cut 1 strip of pink crepe paper along the grain, ⅜ × 4¾ in. (1 × 12 cm). Divide the strip into 3 parts, each 1⅝ in. (4 cm) long. Cut 3 pieces of the paper-covered wire, 4 in. (10 cm) long. Attach the pink pieces at the top of the wires by folding the wire down.

Cut 1 strip of light-green crepe paper, ¼ in. (0.5 cm) wide. Wrap this at the beginning of the wire and ⅝ in. (1.5 cm) down. Glue and shape into an oval, with the widest center section about ¼ in. (0.5 cm) wide. Do likewise with all the pieces. Cut the pink paper down for a smaller detail, only a few millimeters (less than ¼ in).

Attach the 3 stamens around the heavier wire and wrap the base with a green strip, cut against the grain. Use glue. Continue, wrapping the entire stem.

Petals

Cut 1 strip of white double-sided, 31½ × 4 in. (80 × 10 cm). Cut a strip into 12 equal-sized pieces. Lay the pieces in piles of 3 and cup the top part. Cut the petals, following the template on page 146. You'll need 6 of each template. Make sure that the cupping is on the top of each petal.

Cut the details on the top of each petal, with inspiration from the template.

Laminating and cutting the stamens
Cut 1 strip of the yellow paper, 6 × 2¾ in. (15 × 7 cm), and 1 strip of pale-yellow crepe paper, measuring 11¾ × 2¾ in. (30 × 7 cm). Stretch the shorter strip to the same length as the long one. Glue the strips together with cold glue over the compete surface (see page 33). Press the pieces together and even out the edges as necessary.

Apply a thin layer of glue along the top edge of the strip and fold it down ⅝ in. (1.5 cm). Repeat once more. Press it together firmly. Let the strip dry for about 10 minutes.

Cut a fine fringe, leaving a base of about ¼ in. (0.5 cm) all across.

Shaping and assembling the stamens
Divide the fringe into 3 equally long parts. Make the fringe finer by rolling the strip between your palms, with the thicker ends sticking out and untouched. Fold each strip into 4 layers, shaped like an "M," and attach with glue. Attach the fringe below the pistil in an even circle and then press firmly. Use a dowel to ruffle the stamens.

Assembling the petals

Attach the petals underneath the pistil and work for a relatively flat base.

Assemble the smaller petals around the pistil in an even flow. The remaining 6 petals are placed in the space created between the first layer. The second round of petals is placed about ⅛ in. (3 mm) below the first layer. Finally, wrap the stem once more with the green strip.

Sepals

Cut 7 sepals, following the templates on page 146: 5 rounded and 2 oval. Cup the rounded sepals and pull the remaining ones over the scissors. Attach the sepals as a support below the petals, beginning with the rounded ones and ending with the ovals.

Leaves

Create leaves, following the basic instructions and using the templates on page 146. Also see the techniques for leaves and branching on page 41. Each peony needs at least 3 leaves that are joined, but preferably more. When you join the leaves, make sure that they overlap each other by about 1⁄16 in. (a couple of millimeters). Glue along the area indicated by the streaks on the template (page 146). Use the same strip as for the stem to attach the leaves.

Geranium

In a nutshell, geraniums represent the essence of home to me; I love this flower. Before giving a workshop about the famous Swedish artist Karin Larsson's flowers, I created my own variation in paper. For anyone Swedish, her home in Sundborn brings to mind geraniums, particularly the scraggly and crooked ones.

Because flowers growing on so many stems always bored me, for a long while I pondered on a way to speed up the process. The technique is described in the section "Working with a strip on a steel wire" (page 33). When I also clicked on the idea to skip wrapping small, short stems, I hit the jackpot.

I consider the whole more important than the details when it comes to flowers with many stems. One little flower might not look like much, but twenty in a bunch, all together, are completely different. A geranium needs its green leaves. You can choose the slow way in crepe paper, but even hand-painted in regular paper is dynamic. Maybe that adds even more of your personality?

Materials

dark-pink crepe paper (#200) 60 g/m²
light-pink crepe paper (#201) 60 g/m²
green crepe paper (#377) 90 g/m²
white double-sided crepe paper, here, dyed with green watercolors
regular paper at least 200 g/m²
paper-covered white steel wire, 27 gauge (0.37 mm)
paper-covered green steel wire, 18 and 23 gauge (1.0 and 0.55 mm)
paper straw
thread
cold glue such as tacky glue

Prepare the pieces

You will need 15–20 smaller flower stems to create a whole array of larger flowers. For that you'll need 1 strip of 31½ × 2 in. (80 × 5 cm) light-pink paper and 1 strip of 19¾ × 1½ in. (50 × 4 cm) darker-pink paper. For each individual flower, you'll need 1 paper-covered white wire, 27 gauge (0.37 mm), 4 in. (10 cm) long. In addition, 1 piece of darker-pink paper, ¾ × 1⅜ in. (2 × 3.5 cm), and 1 piece of light-pink paper, 1⅜ × 1¾ in. (3.5 × 4.5 cm), following the templates on page 147. Also, 1 narrow bit of green paper.

Fold the strips in piles so you can cut several layers at a time. Begin by cutting straight fringe, following the template. Use a clamp. To round each fringe, loosen the clamp gradually to make it easier.

Stretch the strip of green paper as far as it will go. Fold it several times and cut ⅜ in. deep (1 cm) pointed tips, following the templates on page 147. Use a metal dowel to bend the fringe outward.

Small flowers

Fold the pink strips up and cut them into 20 pieces. Work following the technique "strip on wire" on page 33. First lay the light-pink piece down and apply 1 tiny drop of glue in the center of the fold. Place the darker-pink piece centered on the light-pink piece. Apply 1 drop of glue on this piece. Place a steel wire in the fold and press the strip together.

Press the flower so that you have about ¾ in. (2 cm) left on one side of the wire, then bend it down so the wire is doubled nearest the flower. Repeat for each of the stems. You will also need 1 long, somewhat stronger, wire with which you will repeat the same step—this is the wire that will later become the longer stem.

The stem, small flowers

Divide the green strip with pointed fringe into ⅜ in. wide (1 cm) pieces, with each individual piece serving as the paper for the stem as well as the small sepals.

Apply a little glue along the wire, then press the green piece around it, with the fringe sitting precisely under the flower. Roll the stem between your palms to firmly tighten everything (see page 43).

Assembly

Gather all the stems at the same height around the longer stem. Begin from the point where the green ends, which should be about 1⅜ in. (3.5 cm) down on the stem; this point will be the point for the branching.

Press all the stems together and wrap with 1 strong thread around the branching; knot firmly. Cut a ⅝ in. wide (1.5 cm) piece from a paper straw; cut it up so you can lay all the stems in the straw. If you have fewer stems, you don't have to cut the straw but can, instead, simply insert the stems. The branching point should be less than ¼ in. (a few millimeters) into the straw, so you then cut all the wires except that of the main stem. With the same paper you used for the stems, cut 1 strip against the grain, ⅜ in. (1 cm) wide. Now wrap it over the straw and continue down the stem. Use glue for the whole process.

Fold all the stems out so that they form a shape like a half globe.

Leaves

You can cut the green leaves for the geraniums out of regular paper that is at least 200 g. Follow the same template, but you might want to crease the leaf with a bone creaser (a tool to fold against for a sharp foldline), following the lines on the template. Notch one and the same side on the top of the leaf, so you can fold the leaf into a slight bowl shape. To reinforce the shape, overlap the gaps and attach a wire in between. Another easy alternative is to cut the leaf from laminated crepe paper and attach 1 wire to the back of the leaf. The most time-consuming alternative is shown in the photos.

Cut 1 strip to a height of 2⅜ in. (6 cm). Use the instructions for green leaves on page 147 to cut out 6 pieces. Begin by joining them in 3 parts, with the center one including a wire. Attach the pieces without wire at the center. Cup the leaf upward and place the template on the leaf to help you cut out the outermost lines. Press the middle of the leaf to make it slightly bowl shaped. Bend the outermost edges softly backward with a wooden dowel.

Joining

Assemble the flowers and leaves. Wrap with green paper and glue; reinforce with more wire as necessary.

Iris

When I planted irises for the first time, I had no idea of what would come up. Suddenly they were just there, and it was as if something from another world had arisen from the earth. Still, it is one of the oldest garden plants. When I was about to do this design, I had no real irises in the area. I sat and pondered over photographs and flower books. The flower was so simple in its construction yet still felt more complicated. It is an elegant and sophisticated flower. I think that this has to do with the billowing petals and their uncommon shape.

Materials

blue-violet crepe paper (#380) 90 g/m^2
white crepe paper (#600) 180 g/m^2
light-brown crepe paper (#611) 180 g/m^2
pale-yellow crepe paper (#280) 60 g/m^2
green crepe paper (#368) 90 g/m^2
paper-covered green steel wire, 14 and 23 gauge (1.6 and 0.55 mm)
paper-covered white steel wire, 23 gauge (0.55 mm)
cold glue such as tacky glue

Pistil and petal details

Begin with a paper-covered wire and wrap ⅜ in. (1 cm) with the same blue paper that you will use for the petals. Use glue. Flatten the top with flat-nosed pliers.

Cut 3 pieces of blue-violet crepe paper, following the template on page 147. Cup these lightly and, at the same time, pull upward with your thumb. Attach around the paper-covered top.

Cut out a piece of white crepe paper, 2 × 2 in. (5 × 5 cm), and stretch it out completely. Cut 3 ovals, following the template on page 147. Fold them at the center over the fibers and fringe diagonally toward the fold, leaving a thin uncut line in the middle.

Petals

Cut 1 strip of blue-violet crepe paper, 11¾ × 4 in. (30 × 10 cm). Divide the strip into 6 parts and follow the basic instructions for green leaves. Include 1 white, 6 in. (15 cm) wire in the center of each leaf.

On 3 of the leaves, add an extra line of glue on the lower half, along the fold. Place the white-fringed piece there. Use a needle to carefully press it down in the fold. Let dry.

Cut the leaves, following the template. Make a movement along the edges, following the technique called a wave shape (see page 29).

Attaching the inner petals
Attach the petals without the white center fringe nearest the pistil. Apply an even layer of glue on the back of the petals and arrange them evenly spaced around the pistil in a circle. Press carefully but firmly on the petals, making sure that they attach securely around the stem, so they will sit stably in place.

Attaching the outer petals
Now attach the remaining three petals between those petals already attached. Press on them again to be super sure that they sit properly and are evenly spaced. To increase their stability, you can wrap a thin strip of crepe paper, cut against the fiber direction, around the bottom of the petals. Shape the petals to achieve a balanced and natural look before you continue attaching the sepal. The innermost petals are shaped upward in a vertical direction, while the outermost petals point downward. Bend the petals into a soft and undulating form.

Sepal
Prepare 1 strip of stretched-out light-brown crepe paper and 1 strip of pale-yellow crepe paper, each measuring 2 × 4 in. (5 × 10 cm). Laminate the strips by applying glue on one side and then pressing them together. Cut out 5 pieces, following the template. Work with damp paper. Cup each piece and attach them, overlapping, at the base of the flower. Let each petal successively float downward on the stem, with about ¼ in. (5 mm) space in between each.

Leaves
Cut a piece of green crepe paper, 11¾ × 4 in. (30 × 10 cm), and stretch it out by 75%. Divide the strip into two equal-sized parts. Apply glue with a spatula on both parts. Place a wire on each part and fold the paper double. Cut out an oval along the wire, maintaining the length but narrowing the leaf at the top and bottom. The widest point should be the center of the leaf, about 1¼ in. (3 cm) wide. Let dry and then attach the leaf along the stem with glue. Bend the leaf into a pretty shape. Now look at your iris and adjust both the leaves and petals so that the overall look is balanced. Finish by emphasizing the movement of the leaves with shadows, with, for example, dry pastel.

Cosmos

The cosmos is a simple flower to make, and this version means that you'll be fond of it. The flower is so sheer that I can use extra-thin wire, although it's a taller flower. This way, the cosmos gains a lofty and a somewhat wispy feeling. A variety of colors and shading on the petals create dynamism. By shaping the petals in different ways, you can create both soft, rounded silhouettes and more distinct lines. The cosmos is a flower that you can vary in pistil, size, color, and shape. I promise you that the results will be good; in fact, it's hard to go wrong.

Over the years I've made cosmos flowers in all possible types of paper, but I am most enamored of using the thin 60-gram paper because the surface is more matte than other papers. If you use a higher gram weight, make sure to stretch the paper out before you cut it, following the template.

Materials

yellow crepe paper (#575 or 576) 180 g/m^2
black crepe paper (#602) 180 g/m^2
mixed colors on crepe paper 60 g/m^2
green crepe paper (#962) 180 g/m^2
green crepe paper (#962) 140 g/m^2
steel wire, 18 gauge (1.0 mm)
cold glue such as tacky glue

Pistil

Cut 2 yellow strips and 1 black strip, all 2¾ × ¾ in. (7 × 2 cm). Stretch them out as far as they will go. Glue the black strip ⅛ in. (3 mm) below the edge of the yellow strip. Then, glue the other yellow strip edge to edge with the first one. Cut away any excess black paper on the lower edge. Use a dowel to separate the top of the fringe and let it dry for 10 minutes. Cut a ⅜ in. deep (1 cm) fringe and separate the fringes by rolling the strip between your palms. Make a hook on the wire and attach it at the base of the fringe. Wrap the strip tightly around the wire, holding the fringe at the same level as you wrap. Use a dowel to separate the fringes and then trim them as necessary.

Petals

Cut 1 strip out of the 60 g/m^2 paper, 15¾ × 3¼ in. (40 × 8 cm), and fold it into 8 layers (use a folding guide, 2 × 3½ in. [5 × 9 cm]). Cut out all the petals, following the template. Cut the outer edges with pinking shears or by hand. Cut in piles of 4 petals. If you want to shade the petals with dry pastel, do so now.

Shape 1 petal at a time. Fold it flat, following the technique on page 31. With tweezers about ⅜ in. (1 cm) from the lower edge, pull it upward along the fiber direction with your other hand to reinforce the fold. If you want a slightly turned-in shape, pull a few times at the same time as shaping the petal inward. Finish by pressing with your thumb just above the tweezers for a sharp fold.

Arranging the petals

Glue the petals directly below the fringe, with the glued surface placed below the fold of the petals, about ⅜ in. (1 cm) from the lower edge of the petals. Place 2 petals opposite each other, with a third petal in between them. Place the next 2 petals in the space between the previously placed petals. Attach the 3 remaining petals on the remaining surface by overlapping them.

Cut 1 short strip, against the grain, in the same color as for the petals and secure the lower part by wrapping it around the stem a couple of times. If the glued surface is very wet, avoid adding more glue and let the strip absorb the excess. Let the flower dry for a few minutes so that the color on the stem doesn't bleed into the petals.

Sepals

Cut 1 strip from green paper, 2⅜ × 1¼ in. (6 × 4 cm), and stretch it out completely. Fold the strip double along the fiber direction and cut out 5 points with a base of ⅝ in. (1.5 cm). Follow the template. Fold the points outward by pulling with scissors and twisting the tips. Place the strip on the underside of the flower, letting the tips splay out. Make sure that everything is tightly wrapped around the stem. To soften the transition between sepals and stem, twist the stem back and forth between your palms (see page 43).

Leaves

Cosmos leaves are thin and similar to dill. I add leaves sparingly on a cosmos, following the basic principles. Use 1 stretched-out piece of green 140-gram crepe paper, 1½ × 4¾ in. (4 × 12 cm). Cut, following the template on page 148. Twist all the pieces and fold up both sides around the wire.

Sunflower

Using thin paper for sunflower petals is new for me. Previously, I always used a heavy 180-gram paper, although the instructions are the same as below. When I had an order for sunflowers and wanted to imitate the sunflowers with thinner, more-fragile petals, I chose an obviously thinner 60-gram paper, which worked quite well. The result was a more poetic sunflower, and the process was simplified significantly.

Materials

green crepe paper (#566) 180 g/m²
brown crepe paper (#611) 180 g/m²
light-brown crepe paper (#579) 180 g/m²
white crepe paper (#603) 180 g/m²
light-green crepe paper (#280) 60 g/m²
green crepe paper (#591) 180 g/m²
paper-covered steel wire, 23 gauge (0.55 mm), as well as 9 gauge (3.0 mm) doubled thinner wire, approx. 17 gauge (1.4 mm)
double-sided tape
cardboard
cold glue such as tacky glue

Preparing strips for the pistil

Sunflowers can easily be varied in size with the right method. Increase the height of each strip by ¼ in. (0.5 cm); for double-folded strips, increase by ⅜ in. (1 cm). These are suggestions, but you can experiment; adjust the length depending on the size of the pistil and how many layers you want. For this sunflower, use 5 strips of stretched-out heavier paper:

- 1 strip green crepe paper, 11¾ × 1⅜ in. (30 × 3 cm)
- 1 strip brown crepe paper, 11¾ × 1½ in. (30 × 4 cm)
- 1 strip light-brown crepe paper, 19¾ × 2 in. (50 × 5 cm)
- 1 strip light-brown crepe paper, laminated with white crepe paper, 11¾ × 1⅜ in. (30 × 3 cm)
- 1 strip light-brown crepe paper, 11¾ × 2¾ in. (30 × 7 cm)

I primarily use double-folded strips because they fill out well and mix with single strips for extra dynamism. For these instructions, all the strips are folded at the center, except for the laminated ones, which are single. To control a large pistil, I use double-sided tape. When you fold the strips, let them be somewhat uneven, with 1/32 in. (1 mm) sticking out where the lower edge of the tape is attached. Cut the fringe after folding and make them about ⅛ in. (3 mm) deep. Tape the lower edge.

Assembling the strips

Twist the strips around the wire. Keep them at the same level all around the pistil. When you are satisfied with the dimension of the pistil, cut a circle out of cardboard the same size as the pistil. Glue it on firmly.

Petals

Cut the petals in piles, preferably using a template. You'll need strips 4 in. (10 cm) wide. Depending on the size of the pistil, the number of petals can vary. For the layer nearest the pistil, I use repeated petals on a strip so that the outer row consists of single petals (you'll find templates for both on page 148).

Shape the two variations of the petals the same way. Cup the petals, using your thumbnail to add structure. To assemble, use double-sided tape and create even folds along the bottom. Twist the strips around the pistil so that the tape lies at the same level as the fringe all around the bottom. Attach the single petals with glue, folding them at the same time.

Sepals

Cut 1 green strip out of the 180-gram paper, approximately 2⅜ in. (6 cm) wide. The length of the strip should be 1.5 times the circumference of the pistil. Cut a pointed fringe about ⅜ in. (1 cm) deep.

Begin by attaching the green strip at the bottom only around the stem. At the same time, fold the strip so it sits stably around the stem; press it down firmly.

Attaching the sepals

Now apply glue under and around the entire base of the pistil and up to where the petals are attached. Be careful not to glue the pointed fringe of the sepals. Press the sepals around and outward, toward the glued surface. Follow the fold from the bottom. As necessary, wrap 1 strip in the gap between the stem and sepals.

Leaves

Use the 180-gram crepe paper for the sunflower leaves. Stretch the paper out as much as possible and cut it, following the template on page 148. Attach the parts of the leaves, following the basic instructions for leaves on page 41. Press the leaves together to create structure and attach them to the stem.

Dog Rose

The first time I made these roses was for a bridal bouquet. The dog rose, *Rosa canina*, is a climbing species that's native to Europe and to parts of Africa and Asia. I like that they are single petaled because their skewing is thus close. Roses are one of the flowers that usually ought to be conjoined with leaves on the stem, but in some cases that can seem less important. Take the time to make a pile of petals and then assemble them in sprigs for a large number of flowers at the end.

Materials

yellow crepe paper (#17ES) 180 g/m²
pale-yellow crepe paper (#577) 180 g/m²
pink- or white-colored double-sided crepe paper
green crepe paper (#591) 180 g/m²
steel wire, 18 and 14 gauge (1.0 and 1.6 mm)
paper-covered steel wire, 23 gauge (0.55 mm)
semolina and pigment for structure on the stamens
cold glue such as tacky glue

Pistils and stamens

Cut 1 strip of yellow crepe paper, 2 × ⅝ in. (5 × 1.5 cm). Stretch it out as far as it will go, fold it double, and cut the fringe, 1/32 in. (1 mm) wide, with a depth of ¼ in. (5 mm). Make a tight loop at the top of the wire. Attach the yellow strip by inserting it through the loop. Pinch it firmly with pliers and wrap it tightly around the top; glue.

Cut a piece of pale-yellow crepe paper, 1¼ × 1¼ in. (3 × 3 cm). Stretch it out as far as it will go, and fold it double. Cut a very fine fringe, 1/32 in. (1 mm) wide, with a depth of ¾ in. (2 cm). Narrow the fringe, using the technique of rubbing the whole strip in a pile between your palms (see page 35).

Dip the outermost tops in the glue and then in the semolina. Separate the fringes and let dry.

Wrap the strip for the stamens, with the bottom of the fringes meeting at the same level. When you have finished wrapping, use a needle to spread the fringes out evenly; those nearest the center are vertical, while the outer ones will lean at 45 degrees.

Petals

Cut 1 strip of double-sided paper, 9¾ × 2⅜ in. (25 × 6 cm). Cut out 5 petals, following the template on page 149.

Shape each individual petal by drawing the scissors along the fiber direction to create a slightly banana shape (see page 29). Place your thumbs centered on each petal and cup it lightly. Bend the bottom of each petal outward.

Curl the outer edges in various directions and cut small notches in the outer edges freehand (see page 29).

Attaching the petals

Glue the petals directly below the fringe. The glue surface on the petals should not extend more than 1⁄32 in. (1 mm).

Begin with petal 1 and then attach petals 2 and 3, overlapping them under the first petal. Attach petal 4 overlapped under petal 2, and petal 5 under petals 3 and 4.

Sepals

Cut 1 strip out of green crepe paper, 8 × 2 in. (20 × 5 cm). Stretch it out as far as it will go. Cut the underside for the rose, following the template. Pull the tips of the strip over the scissors to reinforce the outward direction. Twist the outermost ends.

Attach the strip with glue around the lower part of the flower. Fold as necessary.

Leaves

Use the same strip as for the sepals. Make the leaves, following the basic instructions for leaves, using the templates on page 149. Join each rose with 2 sprigs, one of which consists of 5 leaves and the other with 3. Join the leaves, following the instructions on page 41, and do the same when you join the sprigs on the stem.

Delphinium

I have created so many different ways of making delphiniums that I've lost count. Because I always think about how I can speed up the process, I even let delphiniums fall under this technique, which I decided to make public by including it in this book. I also decided to make the flowers all the same size, but to maintain the dynamic, the top flowers are more sparsely spaced than those farther down the stem.

This delphinium has twenty flowers plus almost as many buds, but you can vary the numbers of flowers and colors. Don't forget the leaves, which are important for the overall effect. I consider a delphinium with leaves a complete bouquet in itself.

Materials

black crepe paper (#340) 60 g/m^2
white crepe paper (#330) 60 g/m^2
blue crepe paper (#276) 90 g/m^2
green crepe paper (#366) 90 g/m^2
steel wire, 14 gauge (1.6 mm)
paper-covered white steel wire, 23 gauge (0.55 mm)
paper-covered green steel wire, 23 gauge (0.55 mm)
cold glue such as tacky glue

Preparation

Cut 40 pieces of wire (23 gauge [0.55 mm]), 4 in. (10 cm) long each. To make a full stem, you'll need about 20 flowers and 6–10 buds. For each flower, you will need 1 black strip, 9¾ × 1¼ in. (25 × 3 cm), for the innermost part; 1 white strip, 59 × 1¾ in. (150 × 4.5 cm), for the next layer; and 1 blue strip, 78¾ × 2½ in. (200 × 6.5 cm), for the outer parts and buds. You will also need a green strip, 11¾ × 3¼ in. (30 × 8 cm), and ⅜ in. wide (1 cm) strips in blue and green, cut against the grain.

Fold the strips in piles so that you can cut several layers at the same time. Begin by cutting straight fringe, following the template on page 150. Use a clamp to help. To round each fringe, loosen the clamp gradually to make it easier.

Fold the black strips and cut through the center for the inner single petals. Separate the white strips. To cup the strip, draw your thumb along each fringe/petal. Begin in the middle and draw outward in both directions. You can cup several layers at the same time. Then, cut a strip into 40 parts, with 2 petal pairs in each part. You'll need 2 such parts per flower.

Fold up the blue strip and shape it as for the white strip. Cut the strip into 40 parts with 3 petal pairs. You'll need 2 such parts per flower.

Next, cut 50 single flower pairs; 20 of them will be used for the longer petals on each flower, and each bud requires 3 of these single pieces.

Cut 1 strip of green paper, 6 in. (15 cm) wide, and stretch it out completely. Fold the strip double several times and cut ⅜ in. deep (1 cm) pointed fringe, following the template on page 150. Use a metal dowel to bend the fringe outward. Divide the strip into ⅜ in. wide (1 cm) pieces, where each individual piece constitutes the paper for the stem, including small sepals. Take a little piece of outstretched green paper and cut oval, free-cut petals, following the template on the same page. Draw these petals over the scissors. These are attached as you wish on the stem during finishing.

Single petals

Begin by preparing the single petals. You'll need 20 pieces for the flowers. Place your thumb in the center and twist the lower section. Do the same with the other 20 petals but work them in pairs—these will be used for the buds.

Creating the buds

With 10 of the remaining single pieces, twist each petal once at the center. Press the piece in half in the other one to make a cupped petal.

Shape a drop on one end of each of the 10 wires. Cover each drop by wrapping a blue strip around it until it has an oval shape; use glue.

Glue the cupped petal and the double-twisted petal on the lower end of the drop. Then, cover the wire with a green piece: Apply glue along the wire, then press the green piece around so the fringe lands precisely below the flower. Roll the stem between your palms to tighten everything (see page 43). Repeat these steps for all the buds.

Creating the flowers

Lay 2 blue pieces so they overlap, and apply glue in small drops along the folds on both pieces. Then, lay 2 white pieces, slightly overlapping, on top and apply glue to these.

Finish with the black little petal and apply a drop of glue on it. Place a wire in the fold and press the strip together. Press everything together so that about ¾ in. (2 cm) remains on one side of the wire. Bend the piece down so that the wire is doubled nearest the flower. Pinch hard below the flower to tighten the base. Repeat these steps on all the stems. To create a dynamic for all the flowers, you can vary the shapes by folding out some of the blue petals while keeping others more closed, as faded flowers.

Sepals

Attach the green pieces along the stems. Apply a little glue along the wire, then press the green piece around it so the fringe lands precisely below the flower. Roll the stem between your palms to help everything fall into place (see page 43). Finish by attaching the twisted single petal beneath the flower.

Finishing and the green leaves

Now all the pieces have been prepared, and you can begin the finishing. To construct the delphinium, begin by attaching the buds at the top of the wire, followed by faded flowers and then the larger flowers farther down. Attach a bud at the top of the main stem, ⅝ in. (1.6 mm), and continue to wrap the stem with green strips, gradually including the buds and flowers.

When you attach the last bud, about 4 in. (10 cm) down the stem, add a thicker wire to reinforce the stem. There are no strict rules for placement of the flowers, but the goal is to create a stem that is narrower as you go up and fuller as you go down. I usually create a front where the most flowers are attached, and attach them more densely at the beginning and less densely at the end. Add a single freehand-cut leaf as necessary for extra fullness.

As a guideline, begin by spacing the smaller buds and flowers about ¾ in. (2 cm) apart, increasing the spacing to about 1½ in. (4 cm) for the larger flowers. Make sure that the stem is balanced and that the flowers don't touch each other, by bending the wire. Once the stem is finished, adjust it as necessary for an overall balance.

Make the leaves, following the basic instructions and using the templates. Each delphinium needs at least 3 clusters joined by 3 leaves each. Join the 3 leaves and attach them with a strip to the stem.

Place the leaves in a circle around the stem of the delphinium, about 4 in. (10 cm) from the spot where the flowers end. Bend the leaves over a dowel to soften their shapes.

SERIE UPPRITADE
SKOLARBETEN
LÄMNAS Å RITADE ARBETEN 30%
RABATT.
Serie n:r.
erviettväska 2"
10 x 35
Serie n:r.
"Blekinge
30 x 40
Serie n:r. "Plattsömsduk 1
40 x 40
arbeten
följande
1:65
1:30
Väska
1:90

Red Clover

Giving away a little four-leaf clover as a present is a prosperous sign, if I say so myself. But I also think of clovers as leaves, and making them is a little sweeter compared with other ways of making leaves. Maybe it's because most see the leaves as small hearts. The project below is not for a detailed clover flower but nevertheless creates a fine sense of small pink balls.

Materials

green crepe paper 180 g/m^2
white double-sided crepe paper, here dyed with green and pink watercolor
paper-covered steel wire, 23, 21, and 17 gauge (0.55, 0.7, and 1.4 mm)
cold glue such as tacky glue

Leaves

Prepare all the pieces. The leaves are made partially, following the basic instructions for leaves on page 41. For dynamism, begin with several different measurements for the strips and, preferably, different colors of paper. You can use wire in the leaves or skip it. These leaves are small, and wire is not necessary for the shaping, even if you would have a more stable and durable leaf this way. If you do use wire, choose a thinner wire than usual; 23 gauge (0.55 mm) is sufficient. The wire should be about 1¼ in. (3 cm) longer than the template.

Follow the instructions for leaf making on page 41, but instead of folding in the wire on the back of the leaf, place and glue the leaves, overlapping, with the wire in between. Press together firmly. Let dry and cut, following the template.

Paint the characteristic color changes on each leaf. Arrange the leaves in groups of 3 or 4 so the colors match nicely on the respective leaves.

Join them with the 21-gauge (0.7 mm) wire. Use glue and cover the wires with a wrapped paper strip.

Flowers

The flowers are made with double-sided crepe paper strips measuring 8 × 1½ in. (20 × 4 cm). Fold the strip in the middle, using a ruler for a straight fold. Cut fringe, with each cut about ⅜ in. (1 cm) wide; round the tops, following the template on page 151, and, at the same time, trim the fringe height to ⅝ in. (1.5 cm) on each side of the fold.

Leave the strip doubled and make a sharp fold on each fringe along the fiber direction. Take a 23-gauge (0.55 mm) wire. Fold up the strip and dab a thin line of glue along the fold. Place the paper-covered wire in the fold. Fold the strip over and fold from right to left. Let the strip begin about ¾ in. (2 cm) in on the wire and press the strip together to half of the original length. Follow the instructions for strips on wire on page 33. Make sure that the wire lies as far down as possible in the fold. Use a metal dowel if you need to press it down.

Take 1 paper-covered wire, 17 gauge (1.4 mm), and make a hook about ⅜ in. (1 cm) down the stem. Separate the fringe to create space between the fringes. Hook the strip securely, so that the opening of the fold is outward when you twist. Twist the short end of the stem once around the top and fold it down. Twist the strip around the stem and shift it somewhat downward as you twist. Finally, wrap the stem a couple of times and trim it. Take a narrow strip of green paper and wrap it around; attach with glue.

Joining

Arrange the flowers and leaves in the amount you like. Make sure that you have both 4- and 3-leaf clovers.

Pansy

What I like about pansies is that there's no limit to variations. So, it seems that if you had to choose one flower in all the world's colors and shapes, you would think of pansies. I thought that the instructions for this flower would be totally simple, but it proved to be the opposite. For a long time, I considered what special feature made the pansy especially fine. The outermost little distance between the petals, the knot for strengthening the minimal pistil, and assembling the front petal on a wire were the details that gave me what I wanted.

Pansies are made for hand-painted details. I see them almost as little personalities, as if they had faces. Therefore, I skip green leaves and use the time to paint instead. Try out various color techniques. You can make pansies out of any paper you like. If you use highly stretchable paper, make sure to stretch it out before you cut the pieces, following the template.

Materials

Your choice of crepe paper
yellow crepe paper (#372) 90 g/m^2
green crepe paper (#377) 90 g/m^2
paper-covered steel wire, 23 gauge (0.55 mm)
cold glue such as tacky glue

Prepare the pieces

Cut out the petals in your choice of paper, following the template on page 152. Draw the scissors in the direction of the fiber over all the petals while, at the same time, you lightly cup the petals. Cut 1 strip of yellow paper against the grain, ¼ in. (0.5 cm) wide. Twist the strip between your fingers so it forms a thread. Make a knot in the middle of the thread.

Prepare the materials for several flowers and cut a piece of wire 6 in. (15 cm) long. Cut 1 strip of green crepe paper, 4 × 6 in. (10 × 15 cm). Stretch it as far as it will go. Fold it several times and cut a pointed fringe, ⅝ in. (1.5 cm) deep. Cut the paper in ⅜ in. wide (1 cm) bits, each of which will be used for a stem.

Petals

Petal 1: Fold the topside of the petal along the marking on the template. Take the wire for the stem and dab some glue on the fold to about 1¼ in. (3 cm). Press it around the wire to attach. Let it dry for a couple of minutes.

Petal 2: Place the knot where the first petal ends. Trim the wire and attach with glue on the underside. Attach both petals B against each other as a direct finish to the knot. Take hold of the wire where that petal ends, and bend the flower forward at a 90-degree angle.

Petal 3: Slightly overlap the 2 petals and place them in the connection to the previous petal pair. Leave a few millimeters of space between the middle and back petal pair.

Finishing and stem

Firmly press the green piece along the stem and let the fringe form a narrow sepal beneath the flower. Last, paint on the personality for your flowers.

Acacia

There are many flowers for which reality surpasses fantasy. The acacia is one of those. The shape is fairy-tale-like, and each color combination is more enchanting than the next. If you add petals of various sizes, a single acacia will be a little fairy tale all its own.

The acacia does not belong to the group of individual flowers to create yourself. The construction of the flower might seem difficult, but just follow the instructions carefully and it will unfold automatically. By combining a variety of colors and also working with inner shading of dry pastels, the acacia becomes dynamic in a bouquet. Try working both with complementary colors and colors near each other on the color wheel.

Materials

light-green crepe paper (#558) 180 g/m^2
pale-yellow crepe paper (#292) 60 g/m^2
violet crepe paper (#395) 90 g/m^2
white crepe paper (#350) 90 g/m^2
green crepe paper (#368) 90 g/m^2
steel wire, 17 gauge (1.4 mm) and 24 gauge (0.51 mm)
cold glue such as tacky glue

Stamens

Cut 1 strip of light-green crepe paper, 4 × 2 in. (10 × 5 cm). Stretch it out well. Cut 1 strip of pale-yellow crepe paper, 8 × ¾ in. (20 × 2 cm). Apply a thin layer of glue on the pale-yellow strip. Attach it to the light-green strip, about ¼ in. (5 mm) from the top edge. Fold the strip over the edge and press it together with glue.

Divide the strip into pieces 2 in. (5 cm) wide: Each piece will be a stamen for a flower. Cut a fine fringe, with a ⅜ in. (1 cm) base all across on each piece. Twist all the fringes.

Attach the stamens by twisting them around the top of a wire; use glue. Wrap the stem with a green strip cut against the grain.

Outer petals

Cut 1 strip of violet crepe paper, 8 × 4 in. (20 × 10 cm). Cut 5 petals, following the template on page 153. Shape each petal by drawing it across scissors along the fiber direction. Lightly press the top part of each petal to create a cupped effect. Finally, twist the lower part of the petal.

Arrange the petals in a circle around the pistil. The petals are attached about ¼ in. (5 mm) below the pistil.

Inner petals

Cut 1 strip of white crepe paper, 4 × 4¾ in. (10 × 12 cm). Stretch it out by 50%. Divide it up into pieces 1⅜ in. (3.5 cm) wide. Draw the paper across scissors in the direction of the fibers. Lightly cup the top of each petal and cut out 5 petals, following the template on page 153. Once again, cup the top of each petal. Press your thumb into the cupped section and bend the petal backward.

Place a dowel about ¼ in. (5 mm) in diameter centered on the petal. From that point where the narrow part of the petal begins and ⅜–⅝ in. (1–1.5 cm) downward, overlap the paper over the dowel. Apply a little glue and press down so it attaches. Leave the dowel in until the glue has dried. Repeat on all the petals.

Once the glue is dry, twist the lower part of the cone and fold this part softly outward. Use a dowel to bend the top edge of the petal outward, away from the previous cupping. Add shading in the concave part, using dry pastel.

Joining the inner petals and leaves

The glued part of the pistil is where to attach the inner petals. Attach the white petals where the fringe ends and between the previously attached petals. The cupped part of the petals sticks up between the previous petals, nearest the pistil. The attached surface of the petals should be ⅝ in. (1.5 cm). Leave the twisted part free of the stem.

Cut 1 strip of green crepe paper, 4 × 2 in. (10 × 5 cm). Stretch it out by 50%. Make the leaves, following the basic instructions for leaves and using the templates on page 153. For each twig, you'll need 3 leaf pairs. Make several leaves, varying the sizes for dynamics.

Join the leaves and flower with the same paper strips as you used to wrap the stem.

All templates are at 100% size.

Anemone

petals

leaves for stem

Sweet Pea

folding

outer petal

in-between petal

leaves for stem

pistil

sepals

leaves for branching

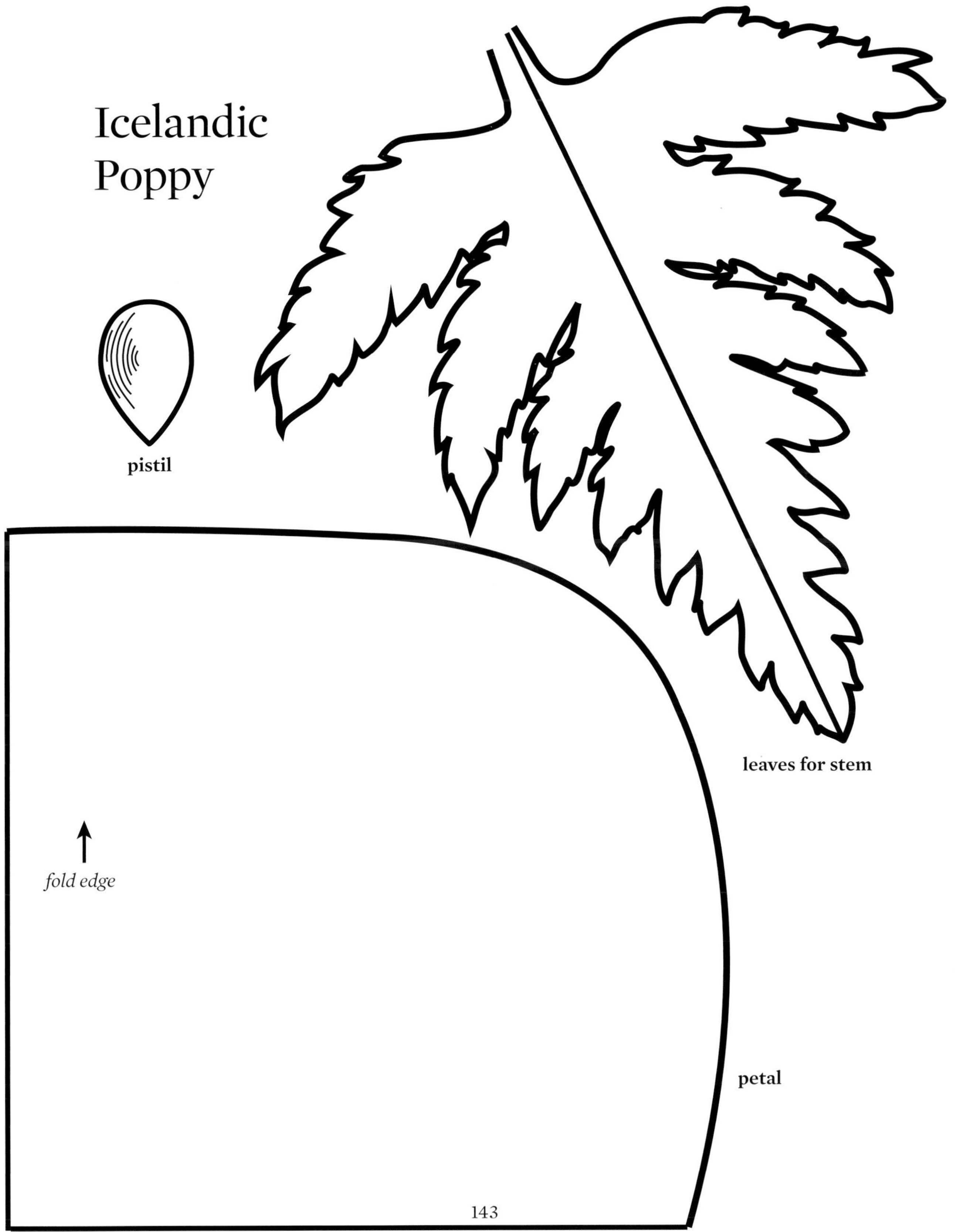
Icelandic
Poppy
pistil
leaves for stem
fold edge
petal

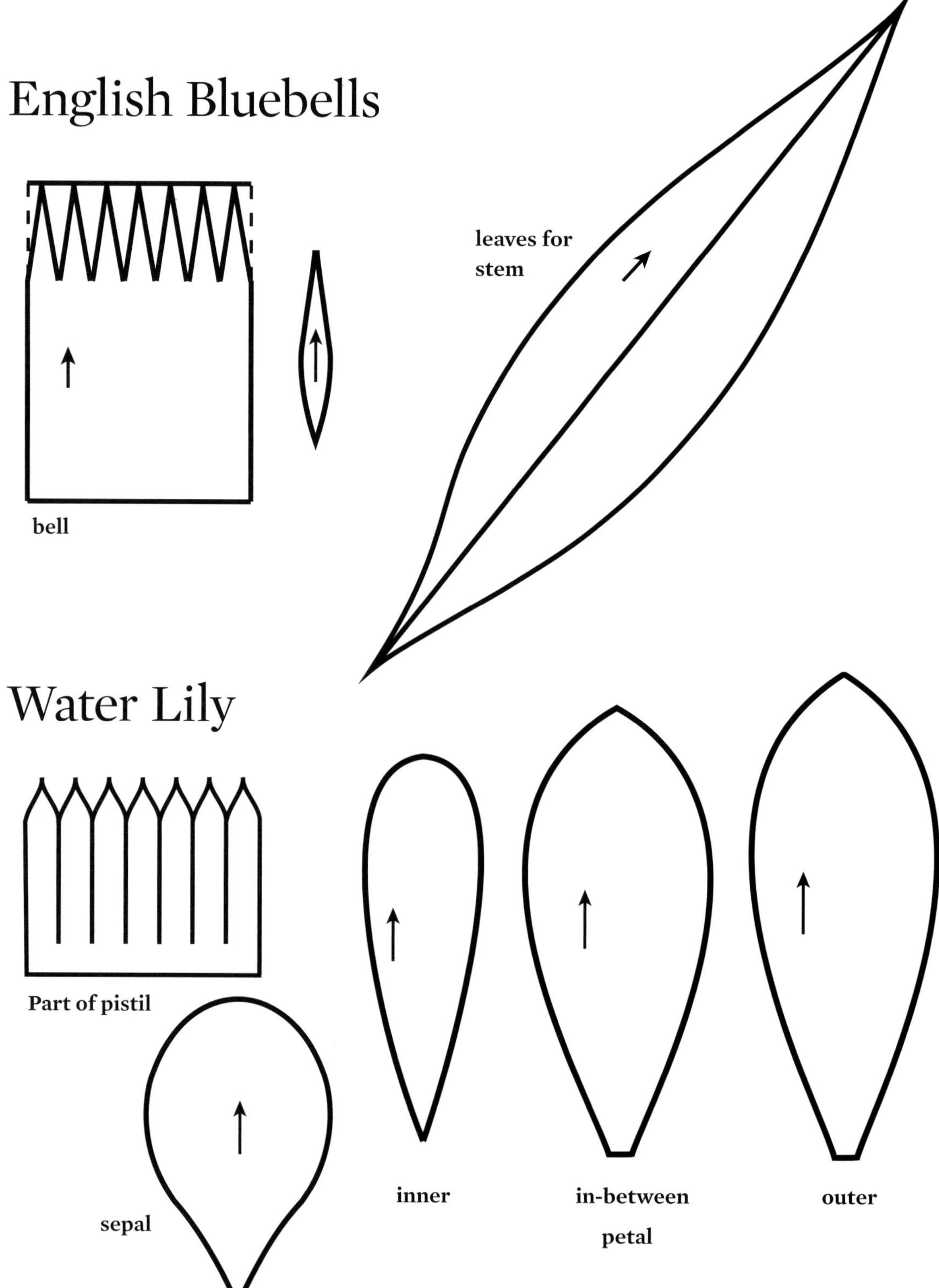
English Bluebells
leaves for
stem
bell
Water Lily
Part of pistil
sepal
inner
in-between
petal
outer

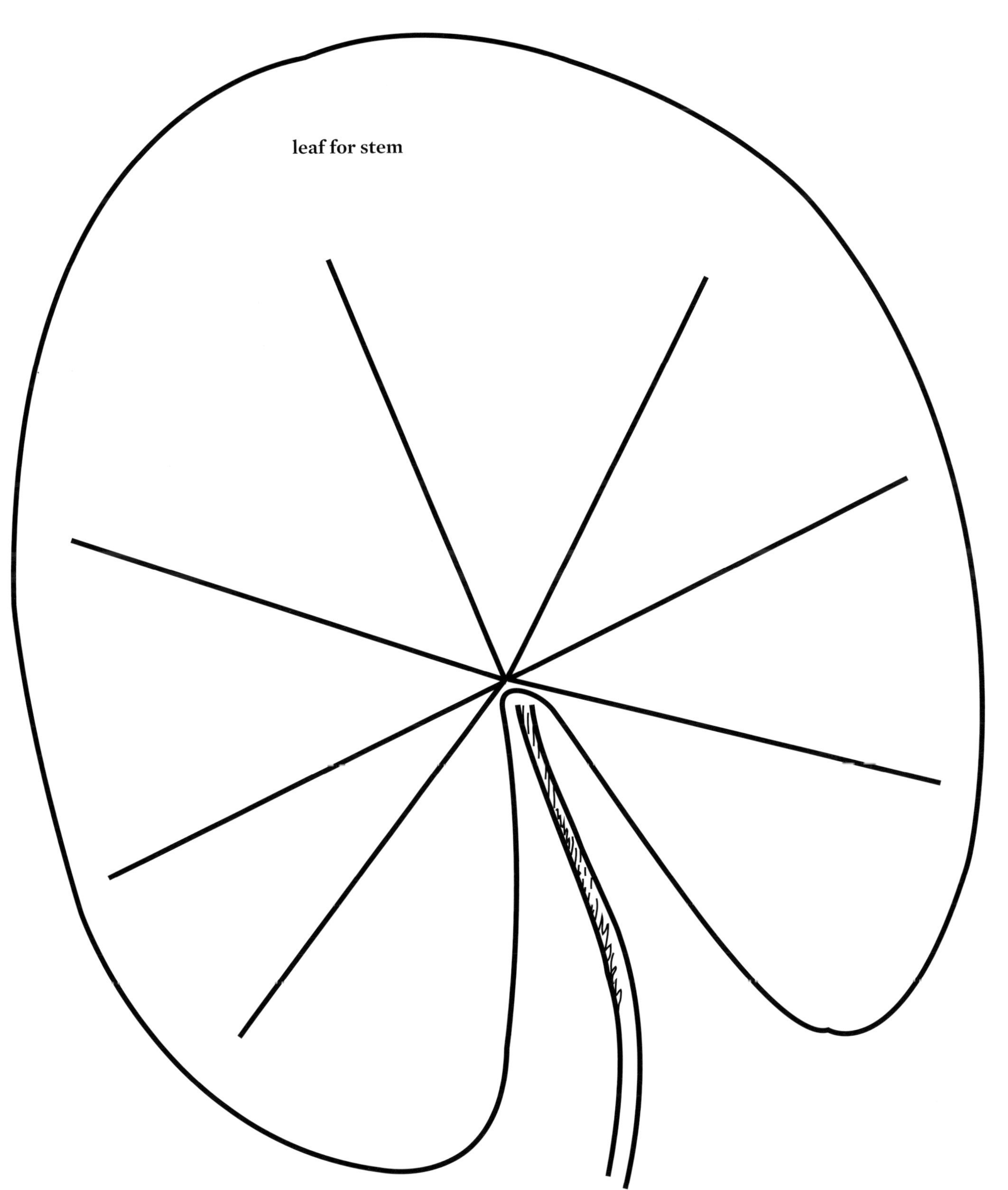
leaf for stem

Peony

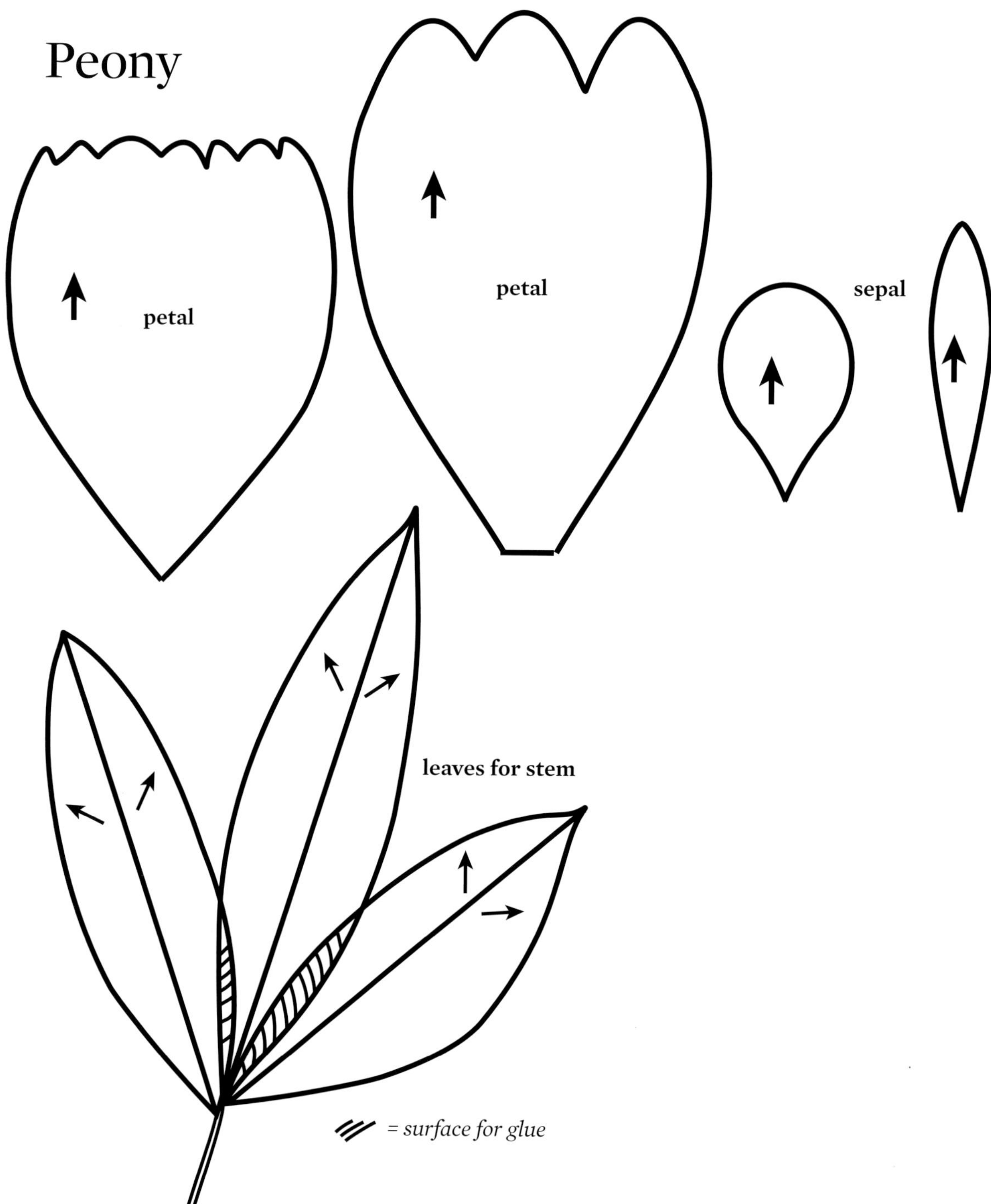

Geranium

leaf for stem
folded edge
outer petal
inner petal
sepals
Iris
sepal
outer petal
detail of petal
inner petal

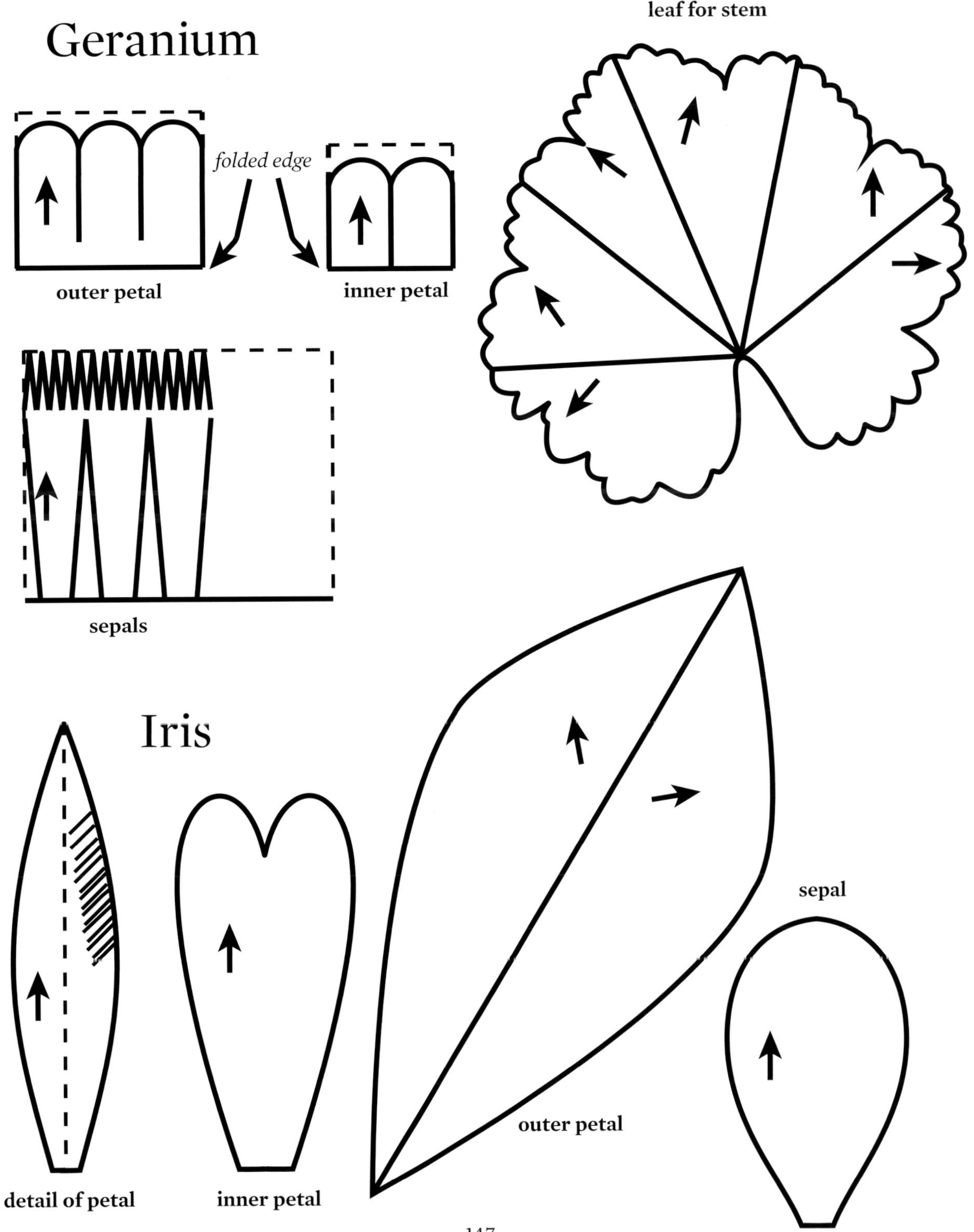

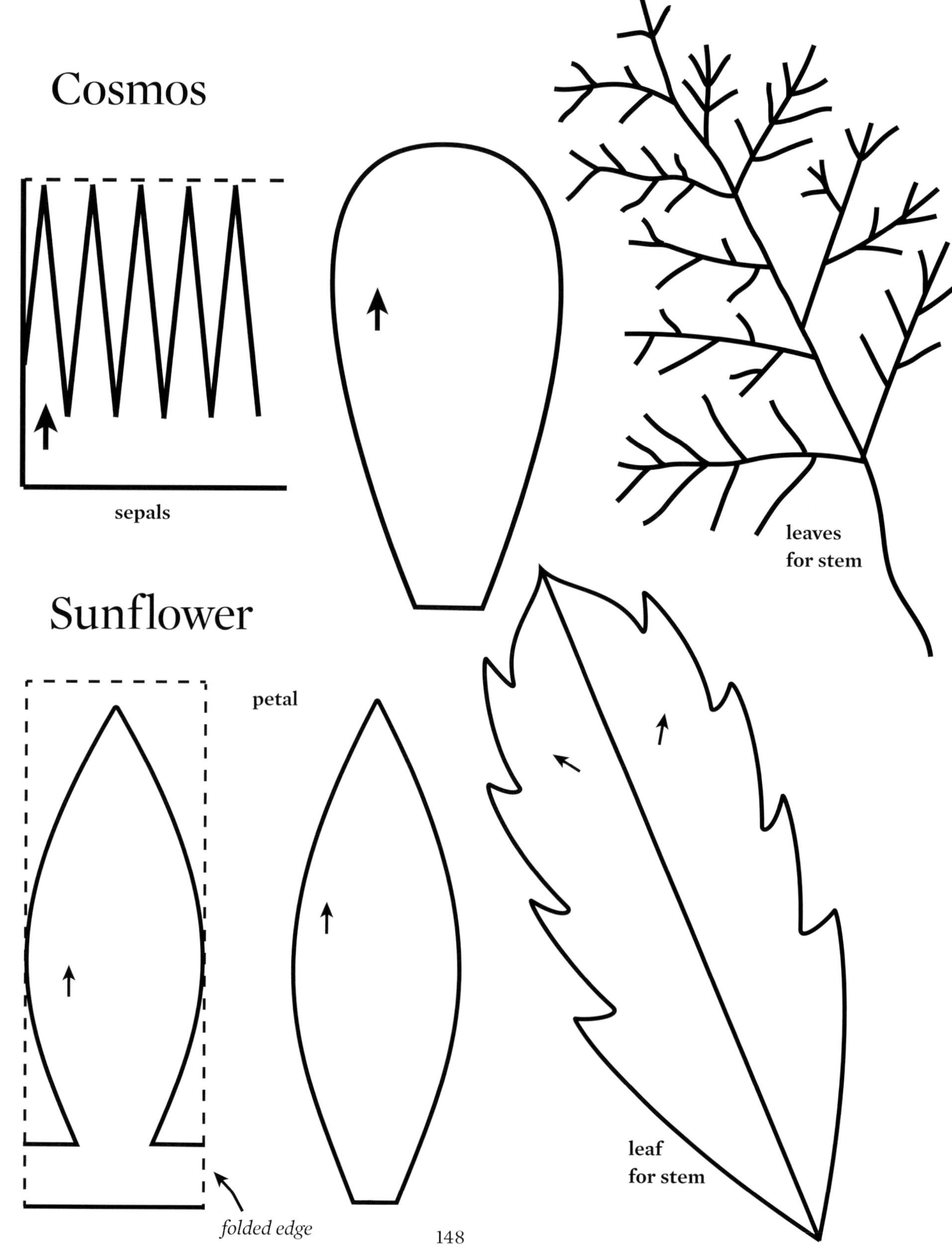
Cosmos
sepals
leaves
for stem
Sunflower
petal
leaf
for stem
folded edge

Dog Rose

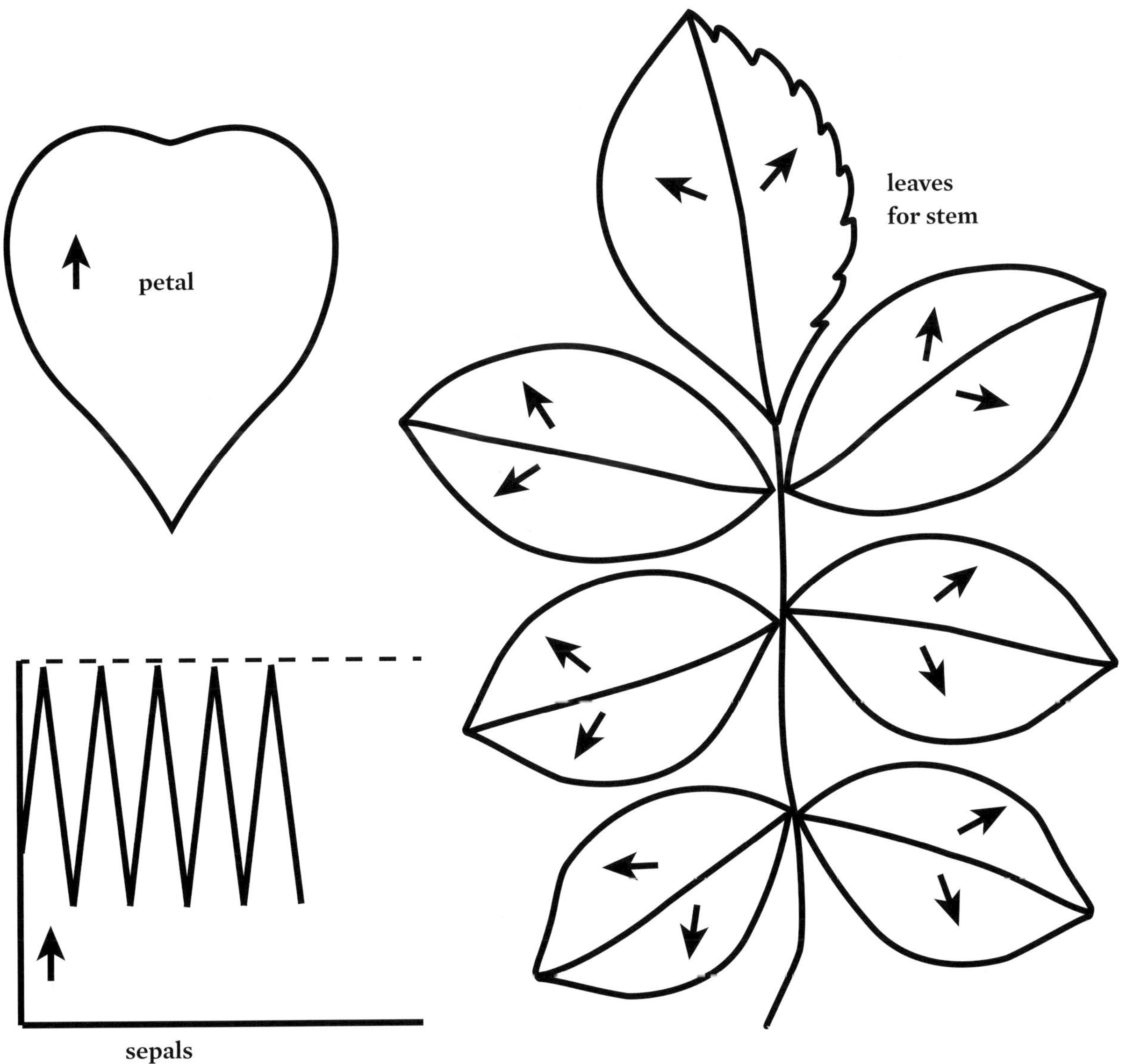

Delphinium

inner petal
folded edge
in-between petal
folded edge
outer petal
folded edge
sepals
leaves for stem

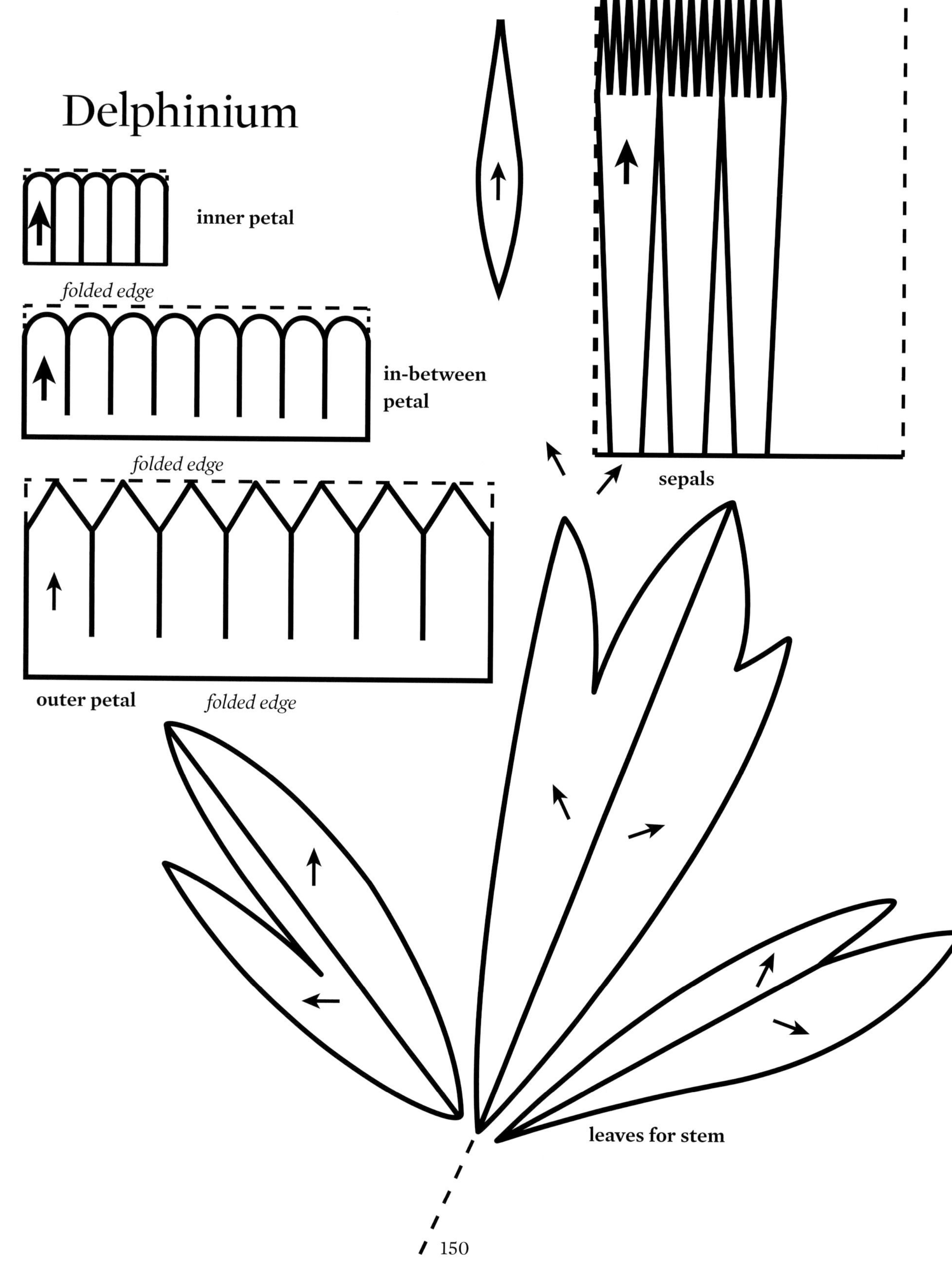

Red Clover

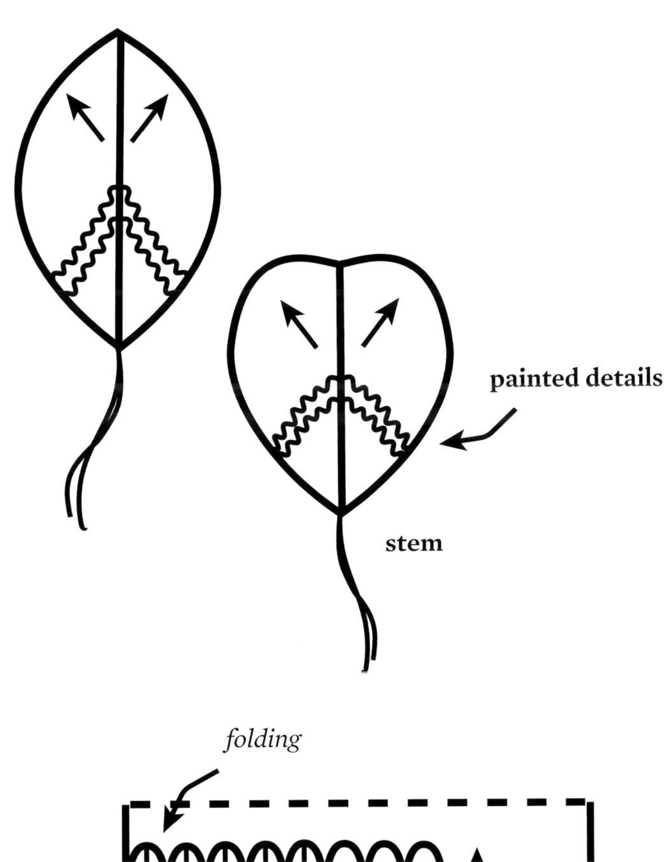

Pansy

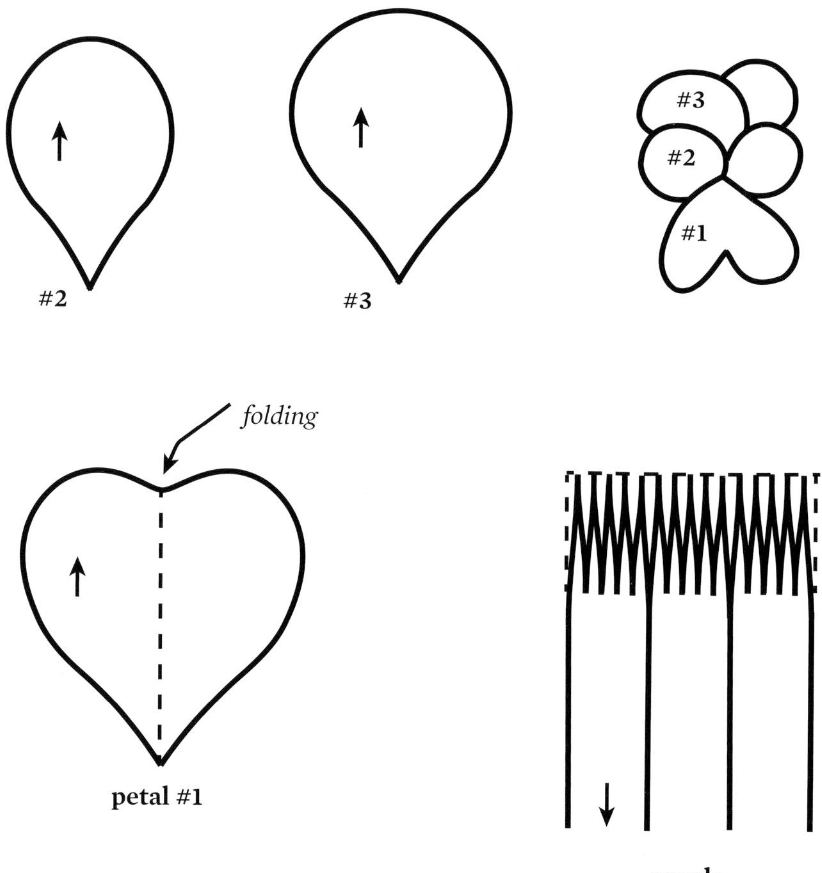

Acacia

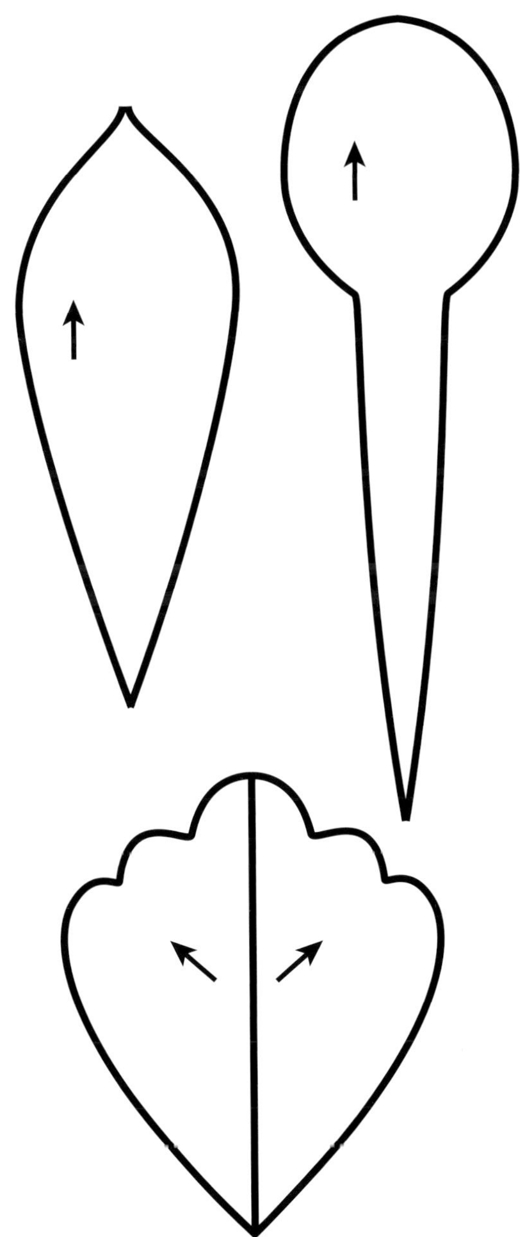

Afterword: Sharing Handwork

Historically, it was common for craft handworkers to keep their methods and techniques secret within their guilds. The reason was simple: to protect their unique products from competition and to limit the spread of their art, which made it possible to control prices as well as the market for their products.

When I first met with my publisher, I explained that I had considered keeping my best tips and secrets to myself. But being secretive had never been my strongpoint. The longer I worked on the book, the more transparent I became. Just as with my workshops, I found it difficult to hold back on anything that improved the process, that made it more flexible or smarter.

What actually was the most basic reason that I decided to share my handwork? To be honest, it's sometimes backfired. I have had workshop participants who copied my classes straight off to create their own course, or who took exactly what I taught and formed their own business.

The answer is this: *If I can help people discover their own creativity, I want to enable it. I actually believe that, as people, we find power, strength, and trust by working with our hands.*

Sometimes I think that this is the strongest incentive I have—when someone tells me that I helped them find a way out of mental health problems, everything else seems secondary.

In 2020, I was asked by Svenskt Tenn (Swedish Tin) if I could design a flower to revive one of our oldest Christmas traditions here in Sweden. In response, I created Winter Light, a flower I made entirely by hand and with a small team that I led. The flower was made in nine steps. Taking a work by hand from idea to production was one of the hardest things I've done, but also the most enriching.

My father, who was also very creative, always supported me in my projects and endeavors, as did my mother. For example, he folded almost 5,000 flowers by using a tool that my husband made specifically for that project.

Two weeks after Winter Light was launched for Svenskt Tenn's Christmas collection, my father suffered a stroke, and a few weeks later, at the beginning of December, he died. This occurred at the same time as the flowers sold out and became a big success. While everyone around me was so happy about the success, I sank down into a deep depression.

A few months later, I was asked to create a new collection of paper flowers for Christmas 2021, but I was still deeply depressed. Despite that, I answered yes. The design process was difficult—I scarcely remember anything from that period, except that I drew a flower named Winter Winds and a lamp. The order was for 15,000 flowers and 4,000 lamps, all to be made by hand. It sounded unrealistic and totally crazy, but those flowers became a healing process for me; that's something I never could have foreseen.

For 132 days, I sat at the same table in our home. I actually remember no details from that time. Every morning, I got up and knew exactly what I would do. People came and went, and every day looked exactly the same. Only individual moments changed shape. I remember that everything was quiet; I didn't listen to anything, and I don't remember anything I thought about. I only know that days passed like the year before, when everything was as usual and my father was still alive. Every day and night, from summer fading into autumn, and finally November.

But when I was finished, on the day after, in fact, I discerned that something had happened in my brain. It was as if I had found a way out of depression, the beginning of a way forward. I had tried everything from professional help and therapy to a range of medicines, but nothing had worked. That the solution should have been so near, in my own hands, was something I hadn't been able to anticipate. The part of myself that I believed had disappeared with my father's death—everything I didn't think I could find ever again—was precisely what helped me.

The monotonous work with my hands was the first step. Those flowers imparted a deep meaning for me in so many different ways. They represented not only the challenge of taking handwork through to production, but also all the obstacles to be overcome along the way. It was also a personal journey.

It was through creating that I found a way forward and discovered that very thing—my creating—could help me and was something I could always carry with me. It was the making, the monotonous handwork, that became the first step. My hands began to once again function with certainty, and this was gradually connected to everything that had broken within me. This was one of the foremost reasons that I consider it so important and meaningful to share my handwork.

At a time when mental health problems are increasing and many are seeking answers and help through various forms of therapy and medicine, I also see how handwork has become steadily undervalued. At the same time as society values mindfulness and increased therapy, handcrafts are often sidelined in favor of industrial, innovative solutions.

But I believe that handwork can be a way back to people's inner balance, a meaningful therapy that gives us something we can't make it through life without. If I can be even a little part of this, I consider it significant.

Projects

Templates

Sofia Vusir Jansson is an artist, handcraft teacher, designer, and author. Since she created her first paper flowers in a large format over ten years ago, her paper flowers have become her signature. Over the past few years, Sofia has made thousands of paper flowers for various collections for the interior design brand Svenskt Tenn and has contributed to several exhibitions at the Sven-Harry, Skansen, and Fredriksdal art museums. She has been featured in *Vogue Scandinavia* and by award-winning lifestyle brand The House That Lars Built, among others. She lives in Sweden.

www.sofiavusirjansson.com
@sofiaatmokkasin